THE AUTHENTIC LEADER AS SERVANT (ALS)

ALS II COURSE 6
LISTENING LEADERSHIP
Attributes, Principles, and Practices

SYLVANUS N. WOSU, Ph.D

THE AUTHENTIC LEADER AS SERVANT
ALS II COURSE 6
Developing Listening Communication Leadership
Attributes, Principles, and Practices

© Copyright 2024 by Sylvanus N. Wosu Ph.D.

Printed in the United States of America
ISBN: 978-1-960224-09-5

All rights reserved. No part of this book may be reproduced or transmitted in any form or by any means, electronic or mechanical, including photocopying, recording, or by any information storage and retrieval system, without permission in writing from the copyright owner.

Bible quotations are from the New King James (NKJV) version of the Bible unless otherwise indicated.

Other versions used in this book are the New International Version (NIV), New Living Translation (NLT), King James Version (KJV), English Standard Version (ESV), and Good News Translation (GNT). Unless otherwise specified, NKJV should be assumed.

The views expressed in this work are solely those of the author and do not necessarily reflect the views of the publisher, and the publisher disclaims any responsibility for them.

To order additional copies of this book, contact:
Proisle Publishing Services LLC
39-67 58th Street, 1st floor
Woodside, NY 11377, USA
Phone: (+1 646-480-0129)
info@proislepublishing.com

Table of Contents

FOREWORD	XI
ACKNOWLEDGMENTS	XV
DEDICATION	XVII
PREFACE	19
About Leader As Servant Leadership (LSL) Model	22
About the Authentic Leader as Servant (ALS)	25
About the ALS Courses	26
CHAPTER 1	
UNDERSTANDING LEADERSHIP ATTRIBUTES	35
Functional Definitions	35
Comparisons With Other Works	40
Principle of Leadership Attribute	42
Authentic Leadership Attributes	43
Summary 1 Understanding Leadership Process	48
CHAPTER 2	
LISTENING COMMUNICATION LEADERSHIP ATTRIBUTE	51
Characteristics of Listening Attribute	53
Principle of Leadership Listening Attribute	55
Summary 2 Communication Leadership Attribute	57
CHAPTER 3	
DEVELOPING LISTENING– PATIENCE	61
Develop patient-humility	62
Summary 3 Developing Listening- Patience	64
CHAPTER 4	
DEVELOPING LISTENING–CONCENTRATION	67
Summary 4 Developing the Acts of Listening- Concentration	68
CHAPTER 5	
DEVELOPING LISTENING-HEARING	71
Summary 5 Developing Listening-Hearing	76

CHAPTER 6
DEVELOPING LISTENING-UNDERSTANDING   79
Developing Active Listening Skills --- 80
Elements that hinder the ability to listen -- 84
Summary 6 Developing Listening-Understanding ---------------------------- 86

TOPIC INDEX   89

REFERENCES   91

Foreword

The modern world today is obsessed with standardization and modalities. As a result, in the realm of leadership, many books have spout associated leadership theories and models and explain them as the path to follow. However, the critical dimensions that distinguish the effectiveness of any leadership process are the values and attribute the leader brings to the table; desired change is influenced by leadership styles or standards. These many standards and theories of leadership often are not in step with the changing times or the followers' needs. The trend is a bit like stocking different kinds of foods in a grocery store and expecting that they will meet everybody's needs the same way and at all times. Aisles are packed with varieties of food with expiration dates in the future, but getting the best deal on the products is what really matters to those who buy and use the products

In many ways, this is the state of leadership in the modern world. Increasingly, even leaders of public institutions are tasked with turning a profit for themselves or the organization they serve. The idea of a "leader" seems to float uneasily alongside the ranks of fundraisers or profit raisers in contrast to any kind of role model for followers or employees. That which is knowable, measurable, and marketable has surpassed the difficult intangibility of strong moral leadership attributes as the central guideline for achievement and success.

In this complicated space, Dr. Sylvanus Wosu introduces his complex idea of the Leader as a Servant Leadership, which is in this book, modeled on Christian tradition. Like all intricate ideas, Dr. Wosu's central point depends on a paradox: a person is best qualified to lead when he or she is most ready to serve. This paradox has been monopolized rhetorically by "public servants" who often serve either self-interest or the interests of specific lobbies. The Authentic Leader as Servant penetrates past the superficial concept of "serving" and details the internal state of true servitude or Servanthood.

While the book is primarily focused on the Christian model of leadership attributes such as discipleship, empathy, affection, and Servanthood, it does so not merely on the grounds of blind faith, but rather via numerous contemporary sociological and business-driven studies on how leaders should seek a leader-follower relationship that is simultaneously productive and nurturing. Dr. Wosu's most piercing insights always involve this secular–Christian dialogue. This book demonstrates that Christ's model for leadership is one that may exist successfully outside the confines of a faith relationship; it places the values of Christ's religious significance in leadership at the center of the framework. It is clear from Dr. Wosu's generous own life story of faith—a faith tested by humbling difficulties—is at the center of both his orientation and motivation for writing.

In language that is so concise, it is often illustrated in mathematical formulas; Dr. Wosu explains the deep structural integrity of Christ's Leader as the Servant Leadership model. One could imagine leaders of any doctrine benefiting from the analyses contained in these pages. The book's message repeatedly encourages the reader to imagine a scenario or reflect on memories and personal experiences to prove or test its many points. Thus, the book depends on a form of praxis, a lesson that could be or has been enacted, by the participating reader. I am very impressed at the volume and level of thinking of the author. Parts of the book involve his personal story, which is especially riveting. I cannot imagine what he had to endure, which he referred to as a" wilderness walk," to accomplish the goal he set for himself. His life stories on these pages are inspiring and stimulating.

In this way, the text eschews dogmatism in favor of the self-discovery Socratic Method of teaching and learning. The reader is not badgered into complying with a religious objective but is rather asked to consider the applicability of difficult biblical concepts in relation to modern life. It is a fascinating and very thought-provoking read.

Hence, the book does not seek to make the leader a servant, a cookie-cutter corporate buzzword, but rather asks the reader to imagine him or herself interacting with a range of concepts. One of Dr. Wosu's great strengths is his reservation when it comes to forcing his reading's interpretation on the material he presents.

The book parallels Biblical and modern leadership scenarios in ways that consistently provoke thought, and while it is clear Dr. Wosu has his particular leadership style; the space for the reader's own thoughts is always left open.

The book could not have been written in any other way with integrity. Its format and formulas are offered to the reader of the leader as a servant role that it analyzes in its pages. To find a text that instructs from this humble position is profoundly refreshing in a genre that is often packaged inside a cover with a sizeable picture of the "modest" author, smiling egotistically beneath a name spelled out in large, gold lettering. Throughout its pages, this text feels as if it serves the reader.

In the end, this is the most satisfying aspect of the book. There is no standardized approach to achieving successful leadership. There is no promise of power and a bigger payday; in fact, the book often proffers just the opposite. The reader is not encouraged to devalue the experience of leadership by finding some economic metric for marking success but is rather asked to think deeply about the most basic elements of internal and social interaction within the framework of a Christian tradition. What this means will be different for every reader. Indeed, even in the context of single chapters, I found myself questioning or re-evaluating moments of my own life. This book serves; it doesn't feel like filling in multiple-choice questions, staring at a wall of flavorless grocery products, or hearing the endless servant promises of today's political scene. It feels like a humble invitation to consider a single paradoxical element of a profoundly productive tradition.

-Tobias Bates

ACKNOWLEDGMENTS

A book on leadership attributes as aspects of Servant Leadership sprouted from the wealth of knowledge and the inspirations of many other leaders. Their writings were sources of inspiration, challenges, and examples of excellence to emulate. I acknowledge the leaders listed below for their help in one way or the other. I am very grateful and I hereby express my appreciation and thanks:

Mr. Wayne Holt, introduced me first to the subject of Servanthood in one of our Stephen Ministerial Training classes, and he is the one who has conducted his life as a leader–servant; he encouraged me throughout my writing;

Dr. Harvey Borovetz, Distinguished Professor and Chair of the Bioengineering Department, is a leader-servant in many ways, he modeled Servanthood and encouragement attributes throughout his leadership in an academic setting.

Dr. Clifford and Dr. Patience Obih, in so many measures exemplified the practical leadership attributes discussed in this book.

Pastor Lance Lecocq, Lead Pastor of Monroeville Assembly of God, for his excellent model of servanthood, empowerment, and emulation attributes to the ministerial team, I am thankful for his motivation and encouragement throughout the several hours on this project;

To my administrative assistant, Ms. Terri Cook, who was always the first to review the manuscript; I am very grateful for her dedication.

To the African Christian Fellowship USA, institutions, and all other organizations where I have served in one leadership capacity or the other, thank you for affording me senior leadership positions that provided the leadership platform and opportunities to grow as a leader.

Dr. Lawrence Owoputi, a brother I am proud to call my friend; for his dedication to serving others, his generosity, healing care, and responsibility attributes during our term in office and in chapter leadership positions; he taught me that excellent following is also part of good leadership;

To Tobias Bates, for his editorial work on the original draft of the book, and his dedication to completing the work.

Mr. Edward F. Kondis, a member of our Engineering Board of Visitors, for his always encouraging and moral support;

Dr. Enefaa N. Wosu, my wife and life partner, for her love, commitment, and prayer support, especially during those long night hours I was not there for her and her constant reminder of who I must be as a leader-servant. Without her support, forbearance, wisdom, and encouragement, this project would not have been completed; I say, thank you very much.

And to God alone be all the glory and honor for the divine inspiration and guidance in initiating and completing this life-transforming book project.

Dedication

I humbly submit this book back unto the gracious hands of God who inspired the writings through His Holy Spirit!

    I dedicate this book to my virtuous wife of 45 years, Rev. (Dr.) Enefaa Wosu whose spiritual leadership is an important gateway to our home, and to our four wonderful children—Prof. Eliada Wosu-Griffin EL, HeCareth, Tamuno-Emi, and Chidinma. From them all, I learnt what it meant to be a leader-servant. I could not be blessed with better teachers.

PREFACE

What characteristics did Biblical leaders like the Apostle Paul, Moses, Joshua, and Nehemiah as servants of their people display outwardly that distinguished them from other leaders, both then and now? The Apostle Paul kept his focus to *emulate* Christ and endured all the infirmities and persecutions he suffered to complete his goal to preach the gospel of Jesus Christ. He inspired Timothy and others through his effective *discipleship* leadership to imitate him as he emulated Christ. Moses' outward display of his *trust* in God's power earned him a good level of trust from the people and empowered him for the mission of delivery of God's children from bondage in Egypt; he had to *reproduce* himself in Joshua to complete the mission. But the greatest of them was Jesus Christ, who humbly sacrificed His life to finish the work of redemption. In His *Servanthood*, commitment, and love for the people, He became the ultimate *model* of a leader as a servant to *emulate*.

Let's consider for a moment secular leaders in these current times! For example, think of Henry Ford, who founded the successful Ford Motor Company; Bill Gates who created the global empire that is Microsoft; Albert Einstein, who in many ways is synonymous with a genius for his contributions to modern physics; Abraham Lincoln, remembered as one of the greatest presidents and leaders of United States; and many others like these we cannot mention. What did all these leaders have in common? What propelled them to turn their initial failures or challenges into eventual successes? None had a direct mentor or inherited any fortune from their parents. Nevertheless, they all eventually succeeded. These people can be distinguished from others based on their self-will to succeed, their self-confidence and belief in themselves, their self-determination, and their perseverance, among other characteristics. The distinguishing characteristics displayed externally in service or relationships toward others are the outward functional attributes that define that leader.

Think about yourself as a student, faculty member, or that new executive. What was it that made your journey to success different and even great? Students and colleagues, when they see or hear about my display of what I have referred to as the 'wilderness walk of faith', have asked me to share the critical attitudinal elements that made me remain inwardly resilient and undaunted and yet outwardly joyful in the difficulties I had faced. This book is the result of those reflections. Let me explain one such teaching moment.

Many years ago, sitting in my research lab on a Saturday morning trying to finish writing my dissertation, a fellow graduate student walked into the room to talk with me. He was contemplating terminating his graduate studies. He was a privileged single male student but felt the load was just too much.

"Sylvanus," he asked, with seriousness in his eyes, "your research advisor suggested that I should ask you, 'what is it that makes you tick?'.'What is it about you that makes you joyful and at peace with yourself and determined to finish, no matter the situations and high expectations we face in this department?"

What he asked me were deeply reflective questions, but I was willing and excited to answer them. Even so, before I do, let's look at the context. At that period in my life, I had four little children as a graduate student; in fact, more children than any of the faculties at that time, except for one faculty member who had eight children. I received little or no support from the department. I was then an international alien, did not qualify for financial aid, and was not given any research assistant position. I was, therefore, self-supported with two off-campus part-time jobs. I joked at being a minority of minorities, the only student in the department with such a label,—but I was self-willed to succeed. My adaptability attribute, coupled with perseverance and resilience, was all that I needed to succeed despite the odds against me. In every exam, homework assignment, or project I had to compete with students with full financial aid, plus they had nothing to distract their attention from their studies. I lived with the attitude that using disadvantages as an excuse was not an option. Aspiring to earn my Ph.D. was a life dream, and I was willing to give my ultimate best to actualize that dream even in the face of challenges. The choice was mine!

So I looked at my classmate and all I could see was a student striding through a valley through which I also walked. He needed me to show him how to walk the walk, to empathize with him. To answer his question, I smiled, not that I wanted to, but because it was just who I was. The joy he attributed to me was an overflow of my appreciation of God's grace that His life in me was externally manifesting His light to bless someone else. It was a great teaching moment; I capitalized on it to tell my classmate that my joy was not about me. He could see physically but about He who was in me, he could not see in the flesh; I needed him to know that I was just showing forth His life in me. At first, my classmate did not understand the spiritual prose or metaphor I was using. He looked surprised but open to hearing more.

I did not ask if he was a Christian. However, right on my desk was my small green pocket Bible. I opened to 2 Corinthians 12:9 (NIV) and handed it to him to read. As he read the passage: "But he said to me, 'My grace is sufficient for you, for my power is made perfect in weakness.' Therefore, I will boast all the more gladly about my weaknesses, so that Christ's power may rest on me," I noticed how absorbed he was in the words

He looked astonished and read it again, this time silently. "This is interesting, but what does this mean?" He asked. I took his question to mean, "How does this relate to my question?

I explained to my friend that the external attitudes he or my advisors saw in me that warranted the question, "What makes you tick" were inspired by my inner value system based on my faith in this same Christ and His teachings. My desire to manifest His life and self-confidence is all because of what He has promised in His word if I believed. I have believed His words and have gained self-determination and faith to make the right choices through Him for my life, and his spirit has given me perseverance and resilience to focus on finishing strong in pursuit of any goal. "With that faith, I have continued, more passionately and excitedly; I can look at my challenges and vulnerabilities and delight joyfully in them, even as an alien minority of minorities! His grace and power have empowered me to do all things I want to do. That is what makes me tick," I explained.

He looked at me as if he got his answer. "Wow, thanks!" he said, looking inspired and ready to face his challenges. As we concluded with a prayer, and he stood up to leave, I pointed empathetically to his face and said, "If I made it despite my challenges, you have absolutely no excuse but to persevere to complete your studies; you can make it too!"

It is fitting to report that this encounter with my classmate transformed his will and determination to continue. Yes, he was encouraged and went on to complete his graduate studies. He emulated self-will and perseverance from the example of the most vulnerable of all students in the department.

The inner value system of a Leader-Servant is founded not only on his faith but his self-will, coupled with self-leadership; it is the greatest mentor who can turn any situation into an inconceivable success. Self-will is the primary driver for determination, resilience, and perseverance. It is what wakes you up in the morning to ask for strength to do whatever it is you are setting out to do. Based on my life walk of faith, I can state with absolute certainty that faith is the unseen assuredness that can empower you to turn your life's probable impossibilities into great and improbable possibilities.

ABOUT LEADER AS SERVANT LEADERSHIP (LSL) MODEL

Looking at the testimony above, do you know the source that energizes the characteristics you display outside and how your inner self is related to what others see outside? What distinguishes you from others is what combines to define your attributes! As a follower, can you identify the characteristics that distinguish your leaders? As an executive, how do you base your evaluation of yourself? Or how do you evaluate that brand-new manager or new youth director you want to hire? To what do you compare the individual's qualities when you look at his CV? What is the basis of your measure? Do you know if you are a substantial leader? These personal questions and much more are the subjects of this two-volume book, 'The Authentic Leader as Servant Part I: The Outward Leadership Attributes, Principles, and Practices', is written in two parts; the second part 'The Leader as Servant Leadership Model. Part II'; deals with the Inner Strength Leadership Attributes, Principles, and Practices.

When we think about today's corporate greed, deepening divide between the haves and have-not, gridlock in political systems, conflicts and wars, high divorce rates, and the rich young ruler in the Bible, it is easy to agree that all these people share a few things in common: self-centeredness, pride, lack of compassion, and greed. There is a great need in today's suffering world for leader-servants who display leadership attributes. These attributes should be oriented toward selfless service to others. Indeed, our world is increasingly drifting away from global serving reality toward the self and apathy. The most credible message or model for a possible solution to this dilemma and the answer to several complex leadership questions can be found in the foundation of the ultimate leader-servant, Jesus Christ. This book defines the Leader as Servant Leadership attribute as the combined acts of two or more distinctive functional leadership characteristics exhibited in service and relationship toward others. There is no better time than now for a book that presents comprehensive and irrevocable facts and principles regarding how to develop effective attributes of the leader-servant.

The Leader as Servant Leadership Model

My first book on this subject, The Leader as Servant Leadership Model, explains that Jesus' servant leadership model is based on the notion of a Leader as a Servant and not on a Servant as Leader. There are four distinct differences between a Servant as Leader (Servant-leader) and the Leader as Servant (leader--servant) models. It is pertinent to highlight them here to connect to this book, Authentic Leader as Servant.

A Leader as Servant is a leader first. The leader–servant as a leader does not in the line of duty go projecting or lording his or her power and authority over others but is the person to lead the process of influencing desired changes in others through his humble example of being a servant or having a serviceable attitude toward others. He or she is a serving leader, not a lording leader. He leads as a servant by putting others' needs above his own needs and rights. Jesus emphasized the word "as" meaning that the leader (the Master) chooses to serve as a servant even though he is the leader. A leader–servant emulates Jesus, who gave up all rights, and emptied and expended Himself on His followers. He empowered them to become more like Him. A leader-servant is known as a leader first but is seen as a great leader by his humble attendant heart and acts of service to others. His greatness comes from his ability to put others above himself.

Leader as Servant is a Biblical Concept. The model or image of a humble serving leader motivated Jesus' disciples to see that if their master could do this for them, they must also be able to do it for others. Jesus clearly demonstrated the process of leader-as-servant leadership. In some cases, He chose to serve by leading when He wanted to create the image or model of the leader-servant in certain acts. In other cases, He chose to lead by serving, when he showed care and empathy toward the people and led the disciples to see empathy as a leadership attribute.

Leader as Servant is an Authentic Leadership Model to follow. The Leader as the Servant leadership model intentionally positions Jesus as an original model of a leader to follow.

He was serving His disciples to demonstrate that the process of becoming a great leader was earned through humble acts of service to others; He made them understand that He was empowering them to succeed Him as leader-servants through service to others. The result was an incomparable legacy of leadership that changed their communities. The fact that Jesus relinquished his rights or shared His power did not diminish His power and influence. In fact, his influence increased at least 11 X 100%, if we ignore the one case of Judas.

The Leader as Servant Transforms Organizational Culture. The proposed LSL model seeks to transform and sustain the community or organization by instilling key leadership values or "leadership presence" among followers or an organization's members. Change is sustained when everyone in the organization takes ownership of the change. Rather than focusing on leading more followers to be great followers who conform to the organizational culture, LSL seeks to lead and empower better leaders to be distinguished leaders and community builders.

There are four distinctions, which clearly differentiate many of the existing servants as Leader-based philosophies in relation to servant leadership from my LSL model. Even in the corporate or institutional worlds, there is nothing better than Jesus on which to base Servant Leadership. There is nothing more authentic and impacting than the servant leadership modeled by the life and teachings of Jesus Christ.

The LSL model uses exploratory questions, scenarios, and graphic visualizations to excite critical thinking in ways no other book on this subject has yet attempted. Several personal testimonies of my wilderness walk of faith with God are used to connect the reader to real-life experiences of the concepts discussed. The riveting effect is that the text engages and encourages the reader to walk through the experiences presented. The aim is to inspire the reader spiritually, mentally, and professionally with this far-reaching exposition on the subject of servant leadership.

ABOUT THE AUTHENTIC LEADER AS SERVANT (ALS)

The *Authentic Leader as Servant* argues that no leadership model is as authentic, other-centered, able to build communities, and productive and service-oriented as the model of our ultimate leader-servant, Jesus Christ. No source can provide a better point of reference than that provided in the Bible. Hence, this book aims to be more than just a text on leadership; it hopes to be a personal discovery for those who aspire to develop effective leadership attributes that grow leaders as servants who ultimately develop thriving other-centered communities. This book presents a comprehensive, biblically-based study regarding how to develop these attributes and how they are applied in a servant leadership process. In this biblical context and for clarity, Servant Leadership means *Leader-as-Servant Leadership*. A *leader-servant* refers to a *leader as a servant*, which is distinct from a servant-leader or servant as leader.

Leader as Servant Leadership attributes are shaped by the Leadership's Inner Value system, which consists of character, motivation, and commitment. The *Authentic Leader as Servant* is presented as a necessary resource to complement my *The Leader as Servant Leadership (LSL) Model*. The LSL model integrates a transformative leadership framework and interactive dimensions of Servant Leadership. Leader as Servant Leadership is a process in which a leader, in his leadership position, purposefully chooses to put others' rights and needs above his positional rights and personal needs. He then serves, enables, and empowers followers for growth that builds a thriving organization. The LSL model looks at the predominant Servant Leadership concepts and shares how they compare with biblical principles on how we should lead and be led.

ABOUT THE ALS COURSES

The three books, *LSL Model* and *The Authentic Leader as Servant* (Parts I and II), together demonstrate that with today's global visions to reach people of all races and cultures, now is the time for an authentic servant's heart of service. Those visions and the leadership processes are most effective with the appropriate leadership attributes centered more on people than on the organization, principles regarding how to develop effective attributes of leader-servant.

The ALS I and II combined presented twenty leaders as servant leadership attributes. The series of ALS courses supply training guide to understand, develop, and practice the attributes in a leadership process. Each course is independent and self-contained and does not depend on completing any other course in the series of 20 courses. It is, however strongly recommended, in fact a must read, that chapters 1 and 2 in each series be covered as they lay the foundation of LSL model on which ALS is based.

ALS (Parts I & II) Course Layout

The *Authentic Leader as Servant (ALS)* leadership (parts I and II) book has been broken down into 20 courses in workbook format to achieve three goals 1) Self-discovery of the acts of developing the attribute under review in the course, 2) deeper understanding of the principles, research and biblical teaching behind the attributes, and 3) Learning the strategies for practicing the attributes.

Instruction

The set of questions following each chapter are designed to serve as a guide to discover, explore, and practice the essential ALS leadership attributes, principles, and practices in leadership process. The questions are comprehensive review based on the content of this specific chapter only.

To maximize the learning outcomes, the learner must read through this chapter and sections. Some referenced scriptures in the book are repeated in the summaries for added review if needed, even though they were discussed in the section in which they apply.

> The exercises that follow each chapter will help you in not only understanding your own strength and weaknesses in your acts of the attribute but will guide you in developing practical strategies you can apply in self-leadership process or helping others grow in leadership
>
> All answers to the questions are contained in the associated chapter or sections; consultation of new sources, except for the reference scriptures, is not needed. Thus, it is expected that you answer the questions after you have read the associated section or chapter of the workbook. The scripture or other references cited are only for references as they already discussed in the book

ALS II Course 1: Adaptability Leadership Attribute—*Flexibility overcomes rigidity in new and changing situations.*

Adaptability is framed as an inner strength quality of a leader in responding to changing needs or situations in a service mission. According to the Army training Handbook, adaptability is "an individual's ability to recognize changes in the environment, identify the critical elements of the new situation, and trigger changes accordingly to meet new requirements." God showed Moses adaptability when he empowered him to use the rod in his hand as an instrument for the mission ahead of him. This course will attempt to give meanings to personal reflective questions to discover the distinguishing characteristics of Leadership Adaptability. Numerous techniques, personal examples, empirical case studies, and applications of the adaptability developing strategies are discussed concepts. Practice questions at the end of each chapter are used to guide your development and to frame meanings out of the content to improve your acts of adaptability in a leadership process.

ALS II Course 2: Courage Leadership Attribute—*Courage is the inner strength of the mind to triumph over paralyzing fears of purposeful action that yields good success*

Courage Leadership Attribute is the lynchpin of effective Servant Leadership that supports the display of all the other attributes? Having the inner strength of character and convictions to persevere and hold on to new and often misunderstood ideas in the face of opposition takes courage—inner strength to triumph over the fear of failure or danger. It is even greater courage to venture into positions or overcome situations that nobody like you, has gone to before or where many better qualified than you had gone and failed. In all cases, they all display courage in the face of obstacles and uncertainties. The success is more about courage than the experience. Can such courage be learned or inspired? How do leaders or successful people in their callings get to their heights of achievements? How can courage be an inner strength within or beyond leadership? How does courage attribute triumph over paralyzing fear? This course explores answers to these questions and more by searching for the distinguishing characteristics of courage. Numerous techniques, personal examples, empirical case studies, including practice questions at the end of each chapter are used to guide your development and to frame meanings out of the content to improve your acts of courage leadership process.

ALS II Course 3: Empathy Leadership Attribute—*A measure of a leader's compassion is the empathic engagement in a follower's experience and state of well-being beyond just expressions of feelings and concerns.*

Empathy attribute is the ability to project one's personality and experiences into another person's thoughts, emotions, direct experience, position, and act toward the wellness of that person. How can a leader walk along with someone in that individual's "wilderness" state of suffering or danger? What motivates a leader to *empathize* with a follower? How is empathy an inner strength leadership attribute? Whether it's in your church, your business, your institution, or in your community, this course provides a comprehensive biblical-based discussion on the role of a leader as a servant in empathizing with those he leads. The aim is to inspire the reader spiritually, mentally, and professionally with this far-reaching exposition on empathy in servant leadership. How can a leader make a lasting positive impact in the lives of those he or she leads? Answers to these and other personal reflective questions are explored in this course on Leadership Empathy Attributes. Numerous techniques, personal examples, empirical case studies, including practice questions at the end of each chapter are used to guide your development and to frame meanings out of the content to improve your acts of empathy leadership process.

ALS II Course 4: Encouragement Leadership Attribute—*The direct measures of encouragement are the inspired strength and quality of uplifted spirit to persevere toward a desired outcome.*

There are times when people want to grow in their potential, want to change their present situation, feel emotionally low in lived experiences, or feel as if they should be appreciated for a job well done. In any of these cases, some encouragement goes a long way to lift up the spirit of someone low. A case study is of the leadership qualities of Barnabas, named the "Son of Encouragement" by the disciples (Acts 4:36), because they saw him as an *encourager*. You can only be an encourager from the strength of your inner personality. The act of encouragement is mostly expressed or *given* to inspire growth or apply a spiritual gift to serve others. What did the disciples see in Barnabas? Obviously, he must have affected them with his acts of encouragement. They saw him as an encourager by his *courage* to *inspire* them at a time they desperately needed to move the ministry forward. This course explores the distinguishing characteristics of encouragement attributes in servant leadership. Each characteristic of encouragement attribute will be discussed in detail with emphasis on strategies of how they can be further developed or practiced by a leader-servant in a leadership process. Practice questions at the end of each chapter are used to guide your development and to frame meanings out of the content to improve your acts of encouragement leadership process.

ALS II Course 5: Initiation Leadership Attribute—*Initiation creates the catalyst for a vision, and the vision when acted upon, produces a desired change.*

The initiation of a process for a desired change is the core of the inner strength of a decisive leader in any leadership process. Initiation leadership is the act of taking step to originate or get something started. In general, initiative is an "individual's action that begins a process, often done without direct managerial influence." The primary outcome of the initiation attribute is that it leads to desired change; something new in the lives of the followers or organization, such as a new growth in followers, a new product or policy in an organization, or a new mission or mission agenda. How do leaders take action to begin a process of change? What are the distinguishing initiation characteristics of leaders such as Moses and Nehemiah in working according to God's agenda? How does a leader conceive a strategic vision for initiation action?. or negotiate his way to influence possible actions toward that vision. This course explores answers to these, and other questions based on examples from Nehemiah (Nehemiah 1:4 through 2:6-8) and Moses and God (Exodus 3 and 4:1-14).

ALS II Course 6: Listening Communication   Leadership Attribute
—*Effective communication occurs at the convergence of listening attention, hearing, and understanding of the information transmitted.*

A leader-servant face three important types of communication at one point or the other. At the core is listening ability as the inner strength and ability to receive and understand the meanings of words and messages internally and accurately in a two-way communication process. How does a leader-servant communication with God, the Holy Spirit, and followers (individually or collectively) to be most effective. The course explores how the three elements—words spoken, unspoken, and in the spirit—offer unique reflections of the communication process and what they share in common. How does listening serve as a critical element of effective communication between people forms the bridge by which a leader can be effective?. A leader's capacity to listen to communicate effectively depends on the leader's inner strength to perceive, hear, and understand the information from written, verbal, and non-verbal exchanges. Each characteristic of listening communications attribute will be discussed in detail with emphasis on strategies of how they can be further developed or practiced by a leader-servant. Practice questions at the end of each chapter are used to guide your development and to frame meanings out of the content to improve your acts of listening leadership process.

ALS II Course 7: Navigation Leadership Attribute—*Leaders who prepare for and chart through a purposeful course of action arrive with their followers at the desired destination.*

The navigation attribute is having a *vision* for the intended destination plus the direction to get there. Having a vision is a quality of the inner strength of a leader and the path that the leader follows in the life journey is often influenced by internal and external factors. The organizational culture and climate collectively combine to make an organization unique through the diversity of employees' characteristics, values, needs, attitudes, and expectations. How does a leader-servant *navigate* and *negotiate* his actions through the organization and people he serves, individually or collectively, to *finish* or *arrive* at his purpose? How do you prepare your followers to *finish* strong or *arrive* at their destinations? This course explores answers to these and other questions and how a leader's inner strength capacity can empower him to navigate the cultural bridges to influence the desired change in others in their personal and professional needs and attitudes.

ALS II Course 8: Responsibility Leadership Attribute—L*eadership responsibility is the measure of the quality of a Leader's accountability for the growth of followers and the organization*

Responsibility leadership refers to possessing the capability and accountability needed in the act of being responsible (trustworthy, dependable, honest, etc.) in a leadership process. At a personal level, it defines the level of your position (pastor, deacon, department head, janitor, etc.) in your church, family, or employment. Responsible leaders in their positions *choose* to emphasize the positive, uplifting, and flourishing side of organizational life. Are there qualities in your position that need to be trained or developed to influence positive outcomes in people and organizations? Organizationally, what are the attributes of the leadership structure, process, and culture that are most conducive for maximizing the growth of followers and organizations in service toward others? How can responsibility qualities be developed to enhance high-quality relationships, emotional competencies, positive communication, beneficial energy development, and positive climates for the effective leader as a servant leadership process? The course explores answers to these and other questions. Distinguishing leadership characteristics of responsibility attributes are identified and discussed in detail. Practice questions at the end of each chapter are used to guide your development and to frame meanings out of the content to improve your acts of responsibility leadership process.

ALS II Course 9: Stewardship Leadership Attribute—*A measure of good stewardship is the entrustments' better and richer growth change at the end than at the beginning*

*Stewardship leadership is the process of u*tilizing and managing the resources entrusted to you by someone. We recognize that God has ownership of everything above, and below the earth. In that context, we are all stewards of what God owns, including our lives but entrusted to us to be managed and maintained in a purposeful manner that will honor God. What are the distinctive servant leadership characteristics of stewardship and how can they be developed? This course explores answers to these questions with reference to servant leadership. Practice questions at the end of each chapter are used to guide your development and to frame meanings out of the content to improve your acts of steward leadership process

ALS II Course 10: Vision Leadership Attribute—*You have a vision when you understand how you get to your mission-purpose and what the future outcome will be relative to your present.*

The vision leadership attribute gives the leader the ability to specify in the present *what* each follower's or group's growth should be in the future, *where* to focus these efforts to meet that growth; *how* he will accomplish all aspects of his mission, *which* future (destination) he aspires to lead the people, and *when* the purpose will be achieved. Leadership without direction leads followers to nowhere. Vision is the most common descriptor of effective leadership and must be clear and inspirational in order to achieve desired purpose. What are the qualities a visionary leader? When was the last time you added brand new challenges to your normal routine to achieve a new you? Answers to these and other questions are explored in this course. The primary characteristics of visionary leadership will be identified and used to frame a principle of leadership vision attribute. Practice questions at the end of each chapter are used to guide your development and to frame meanings out of the content to improve your acts of encouragement leadership process.

Referenced Scriptures

A variety of Bible translations from over 11,200 original Hebrew, Aramaic, and Greek words to about 6,000 English words do exist with variations in meanings and emphases. I am not a biblical scholar and do not pretend to be one; Hence, I have avoided researching the roots of these words and personally prefer New King James Version (NKJV). I have intentionally used other translations for three main reasons; first, to allow for increased impact and alignment of words to the most desired meaning and emphasis in the concepts being addressed. Second, I wanted new and personal discovery of meanings from translations with which I have not been familiar. And third, I wanted to allow readers who may desire translations other than the NKJV the benefit of their preferred translations. Hence, in addition to the NKJV, other translations used in the book include New International Version (NIV), New Living Translation (NLT), King James Version (KJV), English Standard Version (ESV), and Good News Translation (GNT). Unless otherwise specified, NKJV should be assumed.

Sylvanus Nwakanma Wosu

CHAPTER 1
UNDERSTANDING LEADERSHIP ATTRIBUTES

Leadership attribute is the combined acts of two or more distinctive functional leadership characteristics exhibited in service and relationship toward others.

The starting point of our discussion is the understanding of the key functional definitions and concepts that describe the theme of this book. In general, 1 will define leadership as an integrative process in which a person applies appropriate attributes to guide and influence the sought-after attitudinal changes in others toward accomplishing a particular goal. Specifically, the Leader as Servant Leadership is a process in which a leader intentionally chooses to put the follower's rights and needs above his positional rights and personal needs, and serves, enables, and empowers them for desired spiritual and professional growth that builds thriving communities.

FUNCTIONAL DEFINITIONS

In the context of these definitions, I will begin the descriptions of the leadership attributes of an authentic leader-servant by offering a functional definition of Leadership Attributes, and showing how that definition differs from those of Leadership Character, Characteristics, and Traits.

Leadership Character is the sum total of personal qualities in leadership, such as honesty, values, vision, trust, and so on that make up the moral capital of the leader; Leadership character should describe who the leader is inside or the leader's basic personality traits.

The Leadership Characteristics describe the distinctive characteristics or features of a leader, such as attitudes, competencies, skills, and specific experiences that go beyond his character (personality). Leadership characteristics determine how (through skills and competencies) the leader leads or take actions in the process of leadership in any particular situation;

The Leadership traits are the distinguishing leadership characteristics of a leader (these are things that define his leadership characteristics), which differentiate from personality traits... Leadership traits are the set of characteristics that define a particular leader's leadership. This means that a leadership characteristic is a trait when it is a unique characteristic of the leader.

Leadership Attributes, unlike leadership character, characteristics, and traits, is *a leadership attribute and the combined act of two or more distinctive functional leadership characteristics exhibited in service and relationship toward others* or traits externally displayed in action toward others. All leadership attributes grow out of the leadership inner value system but can be externally displayed predominantly as an outbound or outward attribute or both:

1. **Outbound Attributes:** These are distinctive outward-bound attributes emanating from the inner strength of the leader to support external conduct in service and relationships toward others. They form the internal core functional qualities that motivate or enhance the outward manifestation of the inside character toward others. The outbound attribute such as listening and vision, for example, are the direct results of the inner values of the leader such as patience, hearing, love, humility, or all the fruits of the spirit.

2. **Outward Attributes:** These are distinctive functional outward outer visible attributes emanating from the richness of the outbound and inner values of the leader. For example, external attributes such as Servanthood, emulation/modeling, empathy, etc. are outflows from the leader who will directly impact the follower. Outward attributes can be enriched by the outbound (inner) attributes. As shown in Figure 1, the outward attributes in general form the outer core of

functional attributes in the leader as servant leadership, but they can share some overlapping functions with the outbound attributes.

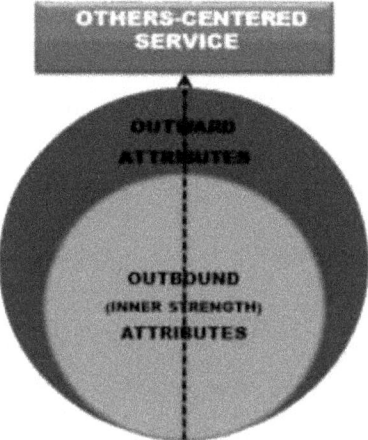

Figure 1.1. Servant leadership functional attributes

In summary, a leadership attribute is more than an ability or a characteristic; it is making those characteristics or abilities functional as part of how the leader acts (his habits) in service to others and applying those characteristics (beyond just having them) in personal and service relations to others. The character or known characteristic defines some aspects of your abilities or who you are inside— e.g. honest, humble, brave, etc. Your attribute, on the other hand, defines your habits; a display of how you use your characteristics, or the actions you exhibit toward others because of who you are inside. For example, empathy as a leadership characteristic becomes a leadership attribute if the followers can distinguish the leader's acts or habits of empathy, such as walking through with his followers in their state of suffering to bring wholeness; otherwise, it is just a characteristic or ability. Leadership attributes toward others are what impact the followers' and the organizational growth more than ability and competence.

In addressing one of the self-righteous hypocritical attributes of servitude leadership, Jesus called leader-servants to be "inside-out" leaders that reflect credibility; indeed, leaders should not appear outwardly righteous when they are full of hypocrisy and lawlessness in their hearts. He was describing "inside–out" as an authentic leadership attribute measured by the display of credibility a leadership attribute!

The measuring stick of a leader-servant is Jesus Christ. We measure ourselves unto the measure of the status of the fullness of Christ (Ephesians 4:13).

The leadership attributes of an authentic leader as a servant are encapsulated in **SERVANT/SERVING LEADERSHIP** are listed in Table 1.1, and defined in Table 1.2: *Servanthood, Emulation, Responsibility, Vision, Navigation, Adaptability, Trust, Listening, Empathy, Affection, Discipleship, Encouragement, Reproduction, Stewardship, Healing-Care, Initiation, Integrity,* and *Persuasion*. Other support attributes include *Influence, Courage, and Generosity*.

The attributes have been separated into Outward and Outbound (Inner Strength) leadership Attributes. As shown in Table 1.1, each of these attributes has three or more leadership characteristics. As such, more than 65 leadership characteristics are covered in these 20 attributes. For example, a leader's Servanthood leadership attribute is characterized by his willing servant's heart of selfless role humility, sacrifice, and submissiveness. The more these are present in a leader, the more effective the servant leadership.

Table 1.1: The functional leader-servant leadership Outbound (Inner Strength) and Outward attributes

	LEADER-SERVANT LEADERSHIP ATTRIBUTES			INNER STRENGTH ATTRIBUTES	OUTWARD ATTRIBUTES
S	Servanthood	L	Listening	Adaptability	Affection
E	Emulation	E	Empathy	Courage	Discipleship
R	Responsibility	A	Affection	Empathy	Emulation
V	Vision	D	Discipleship	Encouragement	Generosity
A	Adaptability	E	Encouragement	Initiation	Healing–Care
N	Navigation	R	Reproduction	Listening	Influence
T	Trust	S	Stewardship	Navigation	Persuasion
I	Influence	H	Healing–Care	Responsibility	Reproduction
G	Generosity	I	Initiation	Stewardship	Servanthood
C	Courage	P	Persuasion	Vision	Trust/Integrity

The list does not assume that a leader has to be excellent in all attributes or even have all of them to be an effective Leader–Servant. However, the more of these attributes the leader displays in his acts of service toward others, the more productive he or she will be, and the further his impact on the followers and organization. The table also shows that two or more attributes can share common characteristics, which can be applied or observed in different contexts. For example, a leader's ability to inspire followers can be seen in his acts of discipleship, empowerment, an.d encouragement attributes in the context in which these attributes apply. Each attribute is exhibited either as a part of the outbound inner strength attribute of a leader or a part of the outward attribute. Table 1.1 is not an exhaustive list of attributes; in fact, there are hundreds of such attributes. This is just the starting point.

Figure 1.2: Servant leadership outward attributes (dark blue) and relationship to four foundational layers of the LSL Model

Figure 1.2 shows that the leader's attributes are shaped and secured by his four foundational layers (leadership inner value system, leadership character, motivation, and commitment). The attributes of the leader–servants are also conceptualized as the support pillars that will establish and support the personal authenticity of the leader, what the leader, does and the effectiveness of the leadership process. Thus, the attributes represent functional pillars of authentic leadership that can be learned or enriched as described in detail in the subsequent chapters. The combined effect of a secured foundation and stable support pillars will make a sustained impact on the growth of followers and the organization.

COMPARISONS WITH OTHER WORKS

The original works by Greenleaf (1970) in servant leadership [1] have been reviewed by Larry Spears (1996), who identified listening, empathy, healing, awareness, persuasion, conceptualization, foresight, stewardship, commitment to the growth of others, and building community as the ten distinguishing characteristics of servant leadership. [2] Russell (2001) has studied these attributes and have shown them to be essential in servant leadership and concluded that these qualities generally "grow out of the inner values and beliefs of individual leaders." [3] Russell and Stone (2002) extended the Greenleaf 10 attributes to 20 attributes observed in servant-leaders. These 20 attributes were categorized by these authors as either functional attributes (intrinsic characteristics of servant-leaders) or accompanying attributes (complement attributes that enhance the functional attributes).[4] The operational attributes were identified as vision, honesty, integrity, trust, modeling, service, pioneering, appreciation, and empowerment with the accompanying attributes of communication, credibility, competence, stewardship, visibility, influence, persuasion, listening, encouragement, teaching, and delegation. Only three of the attributes identified by Greenleaf were identified, and all three were accompanying attributes rather than functional. Responsibility, adaptability, affection, discipleship, navigation, and reproduction attributes which are considered critical in biblical-based servant leadership in my LSL model are not covered by Russell and Greenleaf. As shown in the description of the attributes in Table 1.2, most of the attributes reported by Russell and Stone (2002)[5] or Greenleaf [1] can be seen either in the twenty attributes or their associated characteristics. Integrity and honesty for example are leadership characteristics of trust and other attributes rather than an independent attributes. I take the position that servant leadership attributes are functional attributes in acts of duty to others and emanate from the inner value system of the leader.

CHAPTER 1
UNDERSTANDING LEADERSHIP ATTRIBUTES

Table 1.2: Description of the functional leader-servant outward leadership attributes and associated principles and characteristics

Leader–Servant Leadership Attributes	Principles of Leadership Attributes	Leadership Characteristics
Affection: This is the combined love-based works toward providing the essential help or services for the spiritual growth or survival of another person. . (Chapter 2)	*Affection flows from a person to produce positive emotions for the well-being of another person*	Kindness Compassion Practical Love Affective signs Appreciation
Discipleship: This is the combined acts of personally developing, intentionally equipping, and attentively empowering growth in others to reproduce a heart of service. (Chapter 3)	*Discipleship transforms and empowers followers for service leadership that grows communities.*	Inspiring Shepherding Equipping Developing Empowering
Emulation: This is the combined acts of initiating an authentic servant attitude as a model of service worthy of following (Chapter 4)	*A great leader-servant outwardly and positively inspires a pattern of good works for others to follow.*	Inspiration Motivation Initiation Model Following
Generosity: This is the combined acts of freely sharing with and giving to others as an act of kindness, without expectation of reward or return to him. (Chapter 5)	*Generosity is an outward measure of the level of sacrifice, what is shared, or the impact a giving makes, not just the size of the giving.*	Sharing Giving Kindness Affection Love
Healing-Care: This is the combined acts of providing comfort and empathy to make others whole emotionally and spiritually along with tending to the follower's physical and mental well-being. (Chapter 6)	*Comforting others in any trouble with the comfort with which we are comforted by God, brings healing - wholeness.*	Self-Healing Empathy Reconciliation Comfort Relational
Influence: This is the combined acts of positively affecting desired change in conduct,	*The true measure of leadership success in affecting*	Model Positive attitude Authority

performance, and relational connections toward others-centered course of action or service. (Chapter 7)	desired change in conduct, performance, and relational connections in others is influence	Connection Wisdom Intelligence,
Persuasion: This is the combined acts of communicating perspective to connect, challenge, and convince with a compelling purpose to convert others to a new position. (Chapter 8)	*The means of transforming others to a new perspective is through empathetic persuasion*	Connecting Challenging Communicating Convincing Converting Encouraging
Reproduction: This is the combined acts of developing your leadership qualities in others and releasing them as successors to continue a greater mission. (Chapter 9)	*Great leaders produce successors for legacy and greater courses as an expected product of an effective leadership reproduction.*	Selecting Mentoring Equipping Empowering Releasing
Servanthood: This is the combined acts of humility, willingness, and intentionality in service to others through selfless sacrifice and submission as a servant. (Chapter 10)	*A leader-servant is most qualified to lead when most ready to serve as a servant for the growth of others. The role of a leader is to serve as a servant*	Servant's heart Humility Sacrifice Service Willingness Submissiveness
Trust: This is the combined acts of positive display of character, competence, credibility, and shared relational connections that produce assured trust-confidence of the trustee in the trusted. (Chapter 11)	*True leadership trust produces assured trustee's confidence and readiness to follow based on the credibility, competence, and shared relational connections of the trusted.*	Character Competence Integrity Credibility Confidence

PRINCIPLE OF LEADERSHIP ATTRIBUTE

In the context of servant leadership, a leadership attribute is a level above the leadership characteristic or trait of a leader. The principle of leadership attribute states that every leadership attribute has a set of distinguishing characteristics that make up the inward or outward display of the attribute. The principle reflects the essential designed purpose or outcome of the attribute or the inevitable consequence of the effective practice of the attribute. Thus, the principle of leadership attribute is a concise statement about the fundamental truth, value, or belief about the attribute in a leadership situation; it is a statement that establishes an idea about the outcome of the attribute for guiding the practical application of the attribute and its characteristics. I will postulate and frame each principle as an additive function of the characteristics of the attribute. A statement of each principle is quoted at the beginning or below the title of each chapter. It is yet to be experimentally proven if the attribute is a linear or some other non-linear function of these characteristics as variables. It is expected, however, that each character will contribute to the effectiveness of the attribute in varying degrees.

AUTHENTIC LEADERSHIP ATTRIBUTES

At a personal level, attributes are the value-based inside-out moral leadership assets that can be related to the authenticity of a leader-servant. The complexity of defining authenticity has been noted in the literature. The subject of authentic leadership is well covered in the works of Terry (1993),[5] George (2003),[6] and Shair and Eilam (2005).[7] All appear to agree that authenticity requires self-awareness and objective self-identity in personal and social interactions with others. In his book, *Advocacy Leadership*, Professor Gary L. Anderson offers individual, organizational, and societal perspectives on authenticity: "Authenticity, at a peculiar level, is living a life, whether in the private or professional term. This is congruent with one's espoused values; at the structural level, authenticity has to do with viewing human beings as ends in themselves, rather than means to other ends; at the public level, it is a state of affairs that is congruous with the shared political and cultural values of society."[8]

The basic tenets of these perspectives are very fitting to authenticity as a qualifying element of leader-servant leadership attributes. The attribute reflects how the followers see the leader based on the leader's distinctive features displayed through his or her actions personally, organizationally, and societally. The leader is seen as a leader-servant or serving leader because the followers see him lead as a servant from an inside-out value of others. This is what makes the leader authentic.

Authenticity means that what a leader displays outside, in personal or leadership life of service to others, and society is based on the values the leader espouses inside.

Authenticity in servant leadership can be one or two types or both: *Outbound Authenticity and Outward Authenticity*: The Outbound (outward-bound) Authenticity is the genuineness of personal honesty from your inner strength and abilities; what you say and how you act emanate from who you are or how you feel inside. It reflects the essential truth and honesty about your outward-bound inner strength.

Outward authenticity, on the other hand, describes the truthfulness of your credibility and honesty displayed outward in relation to others; your *outer* visible behavior or how you act outwardly towards others reflects exactly your true intentions.

While *outward* authenticity is the visible *outer* indicator of the truth of who you are inside, *outbound* authenticity is outward-bound attribute from the inside of who you are. Credibility in this context is the influence a leader has to attract believability, trustworthiness, and authenticity; it is the believability, trustworthiness, and authenticity of who you are inside and outside.

A key element of personal authenticity is that it is seen or measured in the context of societal, cultural, and organizational interactions. In that context, achieving individual authenticity becomes a challenge since it is influenced by social factors and dispositions of individuals who usually depend on liberal and organizational realities. However, for leader-servant leadership, the leader can face those changing times by remaining focused on his key Biblical-based principles or *Leadership Inner Value System*. Thus, I am interested in authenticity as an essential element of effective Leader-servant leadership attributes or Leader-servant leadership attributes as drivers of leadership authenticity. With that in mind, the first critical element of authenticity in practicing or developing efficient leader-servant leadership attributes is inside-out self-examination relative to the people served rather than the organization. You may ask yourself: What will be my response when the people I lead act or react in a certain way, will it be negative or positive? What are my strengths and vulnerabilities at those times?

Professor Yacobi in his post, "Elements of Human Authenticity," noted that since "the self -arise attribute emerges from interactions between self, others, and the environment in a complex society and world, there may co-exist multiple complicated identities depending on place and context." [9] He went on to identify the following <u>essential elements of personal authenticity</u>: self-awareness, unbiased self-examination, accurate self-knowledge, reflective judgment, personal responsibility, and integrity, genuineness, and humility, empathy for others, understanding of others, optimal utilization of feedback from others. All of these are covered under the leadership attributes or characteristics shown in Table 1.2.

Bill George, in his book, *Authentic Leadership*, takes the position that to be an authentic leader; a person must have the following essential characteristics: [10]

- Behavior based on value: He must understand his own values and exhibit behavior to others based on those values;
- He must not compromise his values in difficult situations but could use the situation to strengthen personal values in those situations.
- Passion from a clear purpose: Be self-aware of who he is, where he is going, and the right thing to do.
- Compassion from the heart: He must lead from a compassionate heart that allows them to be sensitive to the plight and needs of others,
- Connectedness from a relationship; he must be relationally connected with people he leads,
- Consistency from the self-disciple: He must demonstrate self-discipline to remain calm, collected, and consistent in a stressful situation.

Modeled after the elements above, Table 1.3 lists six essential characteristics of authenticity for servant leadership. These fundamental characteristics cover the five identified above and can also be aligned with the leadership characteristics in Table 1.2. Each attribute in Table 1.2 is expected to pass the personal authenticity test in Tables 1.3, 1.4. In a survey of 132 Christian leaders, seventy-four percent (74%) of them agreed that they always or frequently exhibit servant leadership attributes.[11] Thus, a pass of the outward authenticity test means that a pure leader must demonstrate 70% or more of these essential elements of this legitimacy. (That is, 70% YES in the assessment questions in Tables 1.3, 1.4).

It needs to be noted, however, that a secular leader could be authentic and still lack some of the essential servant leadership attributes or characteristics such as selflessness, servanthood, and love-motivated servant attitudes of a leader-servant. Effective leader-servants are authentic leaders and personal authenticity is an essential element of leader-servant leadership. The key test for leader-servant authenticity is the quality of his inside-out value and personal character. What is most important is a change from the inside-out.

Table 1.3: The test of essential elements of personal inner strength authenticity in servant leadership

	Elements of Inner Strength Authenticity	Inner Strength (Outbound) Authenticity Assessment Questions	YES / NO
1	Personal inside-out value-based behavior	Are your personal inside-out values aligned with acts of service and behavior outside?	1
		Are you honest to yourself in relation to your inner strengths and abilities?	2
2	Inside-out Self-Awareness	Do you have unbiased self-examination, and accurate self-knowledge of who you are inside-out?	3
		Do you know your inner strength and weaknesses in relation to the good you want to show as an outward attribute?	4
3	Inside-out Empathy-Compassion	Do you know and feel from your inside what you want for your followers?	5
		Are you motivated to empathize, based on your inside feelings?	6
4	Inside-out Connection with followers	Do you feel deep, personal, and spiritual connection with your followers?	7
		Does what you say and how you act reflect how you feel when you relate to others?	8
5	Inside-out Emotional Self-regulation	Do you have difficulty controlling your emotion in order to remain calm in a stressful situation?	9
		Are you always able to comfort yourself?	10
6	Inside-out Authenticity Feedback	Do your followers see your inside-out value from your outside behavior?	11
		Will your followers feel that what you say you are is congruent with how you act?	12
#YESs_____; # NOs_____: Outbound Authenticity: YES/ 12-----%			

CHAPTER 1
UNDERSTANDING LEADERSHIP ATTRIBUTES

	Elements of Personal Outward Authenticity	Personal Outward Authenticity Assessment Questions	YES or NO
	Table 1.4: The test of essential elements of personal outward authenticity in servant leadership		
1	Personal value-based outward behavior	Are your personal values and beliefs aligned with your acts of service and behavior toward others?	1
		Do you live out your life according to your beliefs?	2
2	Personal Self-Awareness	Do you have clarity of your personal vision and purpose?	3
		Does what you know about yourself accurately describe what others say?	4
3	Personal Outward Empathy-Compassion	Do you apply how you feel to what your followers need?	5
		Do you lead from a compassionate heart and are you sensitive to the plight and needs of others?	6
4	Personal Connection with followers	Do you feel deep, personal connection with your followers?	7
		Does your outward action toward others reflect exactly your true intentions?	8
5	Outward Emotional Self-regulation	Do you have difficulty controlling your emotions to remain calm in a stressful situation?	9
		Does your evaluation of your value of others agree with how valued they feel?	10
6	Personal Authenticity Feedback	Do your followers see your outward acts as true and honest?	11
		Can your followers see other-centeredness in 70% or more of your attributes?	12
	#YESs_____; # NOs_____: Outbound Authenticity: YES/ 12-----%		

SUMMARY 1
UNDERSTANDING LEADERSHIP PROCESS

Before starting this exercise, please read and follow the instruction in the preface of this workbook. Answers to these questions are contained in this chapter. Completion of these exercises after reading the chapter should take 60-90 minutes.

Discovering the Leadership Attributes

1. What is your alternative definition of leadership? In learning to lead, how would you differentiate the following elements:
   a. Leadership.
   b. Leader as servant leadership.
   c. Leadership characteristics.
   d. Leadership attributes.
2. What are the key differences between the Leader as Servant and the Servant as Leader Leadership philosophies?
3. What was the original source of the Servant as Leader (SL)? What was the original source of Leader as Servant (LS)?
4. What is the key framework of a Leader as a Servant Leadership?
5. Authenticity in servant leadership can be one or two types or both *Outbound Authenticity and Outward Authenticity*: Describe a time when you displayed:
   a. The Outbound (outward-bound)—*outbound* authenticity is outward-bound attribute from the inside of who you are.
   b. *The Outward Authenticity*—*outward* authenticity is the visible *outer* indicator of the truth of who you are inside,
6. Describe the key elements of personal authenticity seen or measured in the context of societal, cultural, and organizational interactions.
7. How are the essential characteristics of authentic leader in leadership process in challenging times?
8. How much of a leader-servant are you? Take the personal leader-servant audit in Table 1.5 to self-assess your effectiveness.
9. Based on the questions in Table 1.5, can you identify each of the twenty attributes? What ones did you score 3 ("sometimes") or less than 3? Review and learn and commit to work to improve.

CHAPTER 1
UNDERSTANDING LEADERSHIP ATTRIBUTES

	Table 1.5. Leader As Servant-Leadership Audit A servant-leader in his leadership position purposefully choses to serve and inspire acts of service in others by his example. Select and circle best answer to questions 1=Never: 2=Almost never ; 3=Sometimes; 4=Frequently; 5 =Always					
	Servant Leadership assessment questions	Circle no				
1	I am willing and other-centered, and readily chose to serve others as a servant for their personal growth	1	2	3	4	5
2	I model others-centered attitude in my service and relationships and inspire same for others to follow	1	2	3	4	5
3	I have a sense of obligation, willingness, and accountability for the service towards others	1	2	3	4	5
4	I have the foresightedness to specify in the present view what others' growth should be in a given future	1	2	3	4	5
5	I work toward providing the essential help or services for the spiritual growth or survival of the others;	1	2	3	4	5
6	I provide the needed purposeful course of action for how to chart the course to for my followers.	1	2	3	4	5
7	I display external credibility and a strong sense of character based on values, beliefs, and competence;	1	2	3	4	5
8	In communication, I attentively perceive and hear what is communicated, reflectively listen to understand and to be understood	1	2	3	4	5
9	I walk through with others in their state (suffering, emotions, etc.) in a way that provides the needed care and well-being	1	2	3	4	5
10	I have a measure of self-secured flexibility to adapt appropriate attitude to serve all people in different situations	1	2	3	4	5
11	I personally develop, intentionally equip, and attentively nurture spiritually growth in others	1	2	3	4	5
12	My act of bravery instills in others the courage and confidence to follow or persevere in a course of action	1	2	3	4	5
13	I develop my leadership qualities in others as successors to continue in a purposeful mission	1	2	3	4	5
14	I manage , maintain,, and account for all resources entrusted to me and being responsible for the difference my acts make	1	2	3	4	5
15	As a care-giver, I act to comfort and make others whole emotionally	1	2	3	4	5
16	When I see a need, I originate a vision and action, and stay committed to meet that need and desired change	1	2	3	4	5

ALS LISTENING COMMUNICATION LEADERSHIP ATTRIBUTES, PRINCIPLES, & PRACTICES

17	I display a holistic view of an issue to inform, transform or convert others to my view through empathetic persuasion	1	2	3	4	5
18	I freely share what I have sacrificially as an act of kindness to others, without expectation of reward in return	1	2	3	4	5
19	My act of influence is to affect the actions, behavior, opinions, etc., of others based on trust, credibility and relationship	1	2	3	4	5
20	In the face challenges and danger, I act with bravery to overcome fear and take a stand with strength and conviction	1	2	3	4	5
Score Range	Add up the numbers in each column (Total Score____ Check and Understand the key areas to work on					
81-100	Strong Leader-Servant; keep it up, go and train others.					
66-80	Above average Leader-Servant; work 25% of key areas					
50-65	Average but developing; need to work on 50% of key areas					
34-49	Below average leader; work on 75% of key areas					
<34	Not a Leader-Servant; need training in all areas					

CHAPTER 2
LISTENING COMMUNICATION LEADERSHIP ATTRIBUTE

Effective communication occurs at the convergence of listening attention, hearing, and understanding of the information transmitted.

A leader-servant face three important types of communication at one point or the other: these are communication between him and God; between him and the Holy Spirit, and between him and followers (individually or collectively). Let's look at each type:

Communication with God: This communication occurs primarily through His written Word. Our faith comes from hearing His word (Romans 10:17) and by praying through our Lord Jesus Christ. "All Scripture is breathed out by God and is profitable for teaching, for reproof, for correction, and for training in righteousness" (2 Timothy 3:16). The Word serves as the primary tool of the trade to equip leaders for good work in God in their fast-paced work. I have seen leaders who have grown so much in the Lord, and they have taken reading the Word of God for granted. There is a sense that they fully understand all of God's Word. The primary function of the Word is to continue intimacy and communication with God. Leaders, therefore, need to read and study the Word diligently, understand what the Lord is saying to them or the Church through the Word, meditate on what the Word is saying, and translate that knowledge into their spirit. The heart of man needs to be guided because it can be "Deceitful above all things, and desperately sick who can understand it?" (Jeremiah 17:9). Only God can understand and transform man's heart. Reading the Word is a way to obey, to "Trust in the LORD with all your heart, and do not lean on your own understanding" (1 Peter 5:8).

Communicating with God is also about letting His living Word speak to and renew your inner man. Hearing the Word of God is part of active communication and listening to God and allowing the Word to minister to us, correct our ways, and guide us in all things. "For the word of God is living and active; sharper than any two-edged sword, piercing to the division of soul and of spirit, of joints and of marrow, and discerning the thoughts and intentions of the heart" (Hebrews 4:12, ESV) Indeed, God has asked us to call on Him to learn about great and hidden things about ourselves and about God Himself (Jeremiah 33:3). Another way to listen to and communicate with God is through fervent prayer to Him. All our prayers are addressed to God, our heavenly Father (Matthew 6:9) only in Jesus' name. That means that we approach God the Father in the name of Jesus, the Son (John 14:13-14).

The importance of communicating with God through prayer is exemplified in the life of Jesus. Have you ever wondered why Jesus, even though He was God the Son, always prayed to the Father? "And rising very early in the morning, while it was still dark, He [Jesus] departed and went out to a desolate place, and there he prayed" (Mark 1:35). Jesus took all the human form, including all the limitations humans experience on earth. He was no longer in heaven, face-to-face with the Father. In His human form, He needed God to help Him in His suffering to carry the cup of the sin of this world. He was also about the Father's agenda. How else could He have done it better except to be in constant communication with the Father in Heaven? Hence, Jesus fervently prayed to connect continually with the Father. The vivid lesson that we the mortal leaders must learn daily, (Thessalonians 5:17) is to communicate with God to build closer intimacy with Him fervently, and without ceasing. Leaders often do not receive from God what they need because they do not ask. And, when they ask, they do it for the wrong motives (James 4:2-3) or have unforgiving hearts.

Communication with the Holy Spirit: The Holy Spirit guides us in all things, including communicating with God and helping us remember all the Lord has promised to do and all that we are committed to do in His name (John 14:26). The Holy Spirit functions as the leader's constant, invisible accountability partner, always convicting him of sin (John 16:7-11) while guiding him to all truth (John 16:13). The Spirit also communicates with and reassures our inner man that we are His and are on the right path with Him. The Spirit is also the leader's messenger to the Father, interceding, communicating, and pleading with the Father on our behalf; He is the leader's ultimate comforter when he is weary, heavy-hearted, and unable to pray for himself (Romans 8:26). We live in the Spirit and are therefore expected to walk in the Spirit so that we can overcome sin (Galatians 5:25).

Communication with followers: Communication (written, verbal, and non-verbal) with followers is the primary mode of influence in your leadership. The primary goals of two-way communication are to inform, educate, convince, persuade, and influence actions. Think about the interrelated nature of concentration, hearing, and understanding communication by imagining a two-way telephone conversion between two people or one person and a group. Imagine trying to have such a conversion in a party-hall full of people, in a railway station with a train passing, or areas with poor reception. Interruptions between the two parties involved, poor perceptions (which in this case could be prejudiced or subjective), and the environment could all hinder the ability to concentrate, hear, and understand the words spoken or to sense the emotions within the words. Unless we hear by paying attention and have mutual understanding, listening will not occur and will not result in communication.

CHARACTERISTICS OF LISTENING ATTRIBUTE

Listening is the inner strength and ability to receive and understand the meanings of words and messages internally and accurately in a two-way communication process. The communication process involves the exchange of information between two parties or transferring of information or messages from one point to another. Any of the three types of communication above involves the ability to talk, hear, listen, and understand. This talk may be verbal, non-verbal, or simply meditating in your spirit. It is a two-way communication; listening in such a communication process between two people or between a person and a group of people requires *patience, attention, concentration,* and *hearing* (with understanding) and involves the active participation of all the people in the process. Communication breaks down when the intended message is misunderstood or when information is missing in what is being communicated.

Figure 6.1 illustrates the interrelatedness of the three elements related to words involved in empathetic communication:

(1) *Content*— made up of the; who what, why, and how, - in relation to what the follower is saying. The content comes in the words spoken in the communication.

(2) *Feelings*— revealed from the unspoken or expressed reasons and emotions behind the content and come from the words within the spirit; feelings communicate the emotions expressed in the content.

(3) *Spiritual concern*— the hopes, questions, or joys caused by the situation or oppressions outside God. Spiritual concerns are embedded both in the content and feeling and are the spiritual elements in communication.

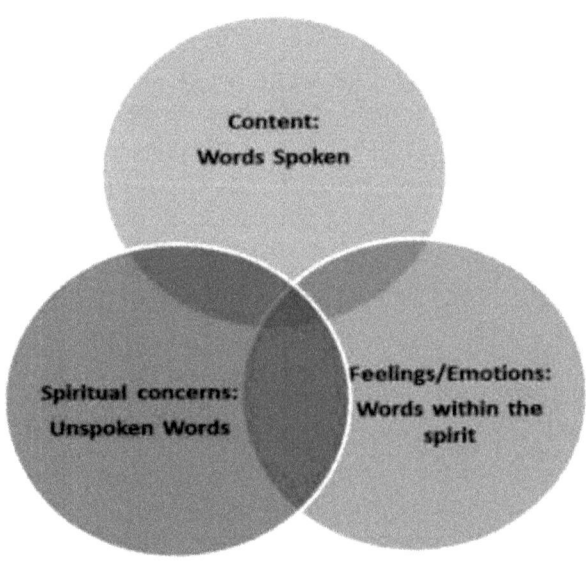

Figure 6.1: Interrelatedness of three elements of Empathetic –listening

Chapter 2
Listening Communication Leadership Attribute

Imagine a leader-servant as a *receiver* (R) communicating with a follower, which I call a *transmitter* (T). The follower is in a state of suffering, with difficulties or impending danger. For example, communication between Mr. R and Mr. T could be illustrated as follows:

Consider this framework (statement by a follower (T)): What happened was (content)…and caused us to (spiritual concerns)… which is why we feel (feelings)…

Mr. T narrated a situation at home about a problem he was having with his son and how (content) it was tearing (effect) the family unity apart (spiritual concern). The situation was also causing (spiritual concerns) and conflict between Mr. T and his wife. He used coded words to hide his true feelings. Mr. R reflected back to him that his wife was a part of the conflict, but he never mentioned anything about her directly.

"What does your wife say about the situation?" I asked Mr. R.

"Oh no, do not even bring her in," said Mr. T. "She simply supports our son and does not respect my opinion on this." Mr. T was clearly enraged; his hands were shaking, and his eyes were red (anger within the spirit).

It is clear in this example that the core of Mr. T's problem is more with his wife's differing perspective on the situation than with his son's behavior. The leader's challenge is to know how to reflectively deal with those unspoken words to decode the feelings that usually cause barriers to effective communication and healthy relationships.

PRINCIPLE OF LEADERSHIP LISTENING ATTRIBUTE

Although all three elements—words spoken, unspoken, and in the spirit—offer unique reflections of the communication process, they share things in common. In particular, the primary focus falls on an effective understanding of the information communicated. The three levels and associated characteristics required to reach effective listening communication are: *patience, concentrated listening, hearing listening,* and *understanding listening.* Hence the definition:

Servant leadership listening attribute is the combined acts of attentively hearing what is being communicated, reflectively attending to understand, and empathically responding to connect emotionally.

Listening as a critical element of effective communication between people forms the bridge by which a leader can be effective. A leader's capacity to listen to communicate effectively depends on the leader's inner strength to perceive, hear, and understand the information from written, verbal, and non-verbal exchanges. The principle is stated as follows:

Servant Leadership listening principle: Effective communication occurs at the convergence of listening attention, hearing, and understanding of the information transmitted,

This principle can be expressed as the following linear additive effect of the acts of concentrating, hearing, and understanding:

PATIENCE + CONCENTRATION + HEARING + UNDERSTANDING = LISTENING

This principle means that the leader-servant's good listening skills must benefit the personal lives of the followers, including their social capital, self-confidence, better health, increased mutual understanding, and growth. The principle also means that listening communication is a critical mark of a caring leader. Without effective listening attributes, communication with followers will fail as information transmitted could be lost due to negligence in any of these three elements. In the business world, good listening skills lead to **better customer satisfaction, greater productivity, increased sharing of information, and better decision-making**. Figure 6.2 shows that as the people in a communication engagement pay more attention, effective optimal communication occurs at the point of the greatest attention with maximum understanding.

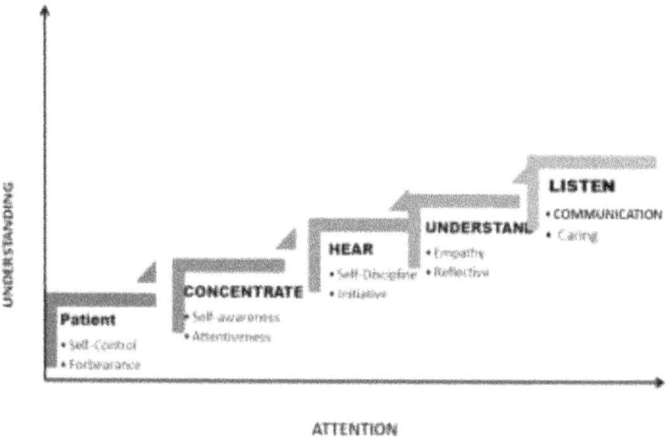

Figure 6.2: The four basic levels of effective listening ommunication

SUMMARY 2
COMMUNICATION LEADERSHIP ATTRIBUTE

Before starting this exercise, please read and follow the instruction in the preface of this workbook. Answers to these questions are contained in this chapter. Completion of these exercises after reading the chapter should take 60-90 minutes.

Discovering Listening-Communication Attribute

1. What are the three important types of communication a leader faces at one point or between him and God; between him and the Holy Spirit, and between him and followers (individually or collectively? How are these types of communications different from each other?
2. What would you consider the key characteristics of the listening communication leadership attribute?
3. What are the three elements of listening communication and how are they empathetically interrelated

4. What are the pathways of Communication with God? What does the Bible teach about such communication? (See Romans 10:17; 2 Timothy 3:16; 1 Peter 5:8; (Hebrews 4:12, ESV) (Matthew 6:9)
5. Take the leader-servant listening-communication audit in Table AII.6. Based on the questions in Table AII.6, can you identify the key characteristics of listening-communication? What ones did you score 3 ("sometimes") or less than 3
6. With reference to listening-communication leadership attribute, what take-away, meaning or lesson can you frame to improve your acts of effective listening -communication in a leadership process?
7. Write a personal commitment how to improve

Understanding the Principle of Listening-Communication

1. State the Principle of Leadership Listening Attribute based on the three elements you identified.
2. How do define *Servant leadership listening attribute?*
3. How is Listening as a critical element of effective communication between people
4. State the additive law of Principle of Leadership Listening Attribute
5. What value or meaning does this principle add in a leadership process

Practicing Listening -Communication Attribute

1. How many acts of listening as an attribute do you display? Take the leadership listening Attribute audit in Table AII.6
2. What are the types of listening involved in communications?
3. How does communication with God occur?
4. What are the primary goals in Communication with Followers?
5. How did Jesus exemplify importance of communicating with God through prayer (Mark 1:35; Thessalonians 5:17; John 14:13-14).
6. What did the Bible teach about Communication with the Holy Spirit?: (John 14:26; John 16:7-11)
7. What is the primary goal of two-way Communication with followers?
8. With reference to listening-communication leadership attribute, what take-away, meaning or lesson can you frame to improve your acts of listening-communication in a leadership process?
9. Write a commitment statement for plan to improve

CHAPTER 2
LISTENING COMMUNICATION LEADERSHIP ATTRIBUTE

Table AII. 6. Listening Attribute Audit
Understanding the Health of your communication

Servant leadership listening attribute id the combined acts of attentively hearing what is being communicated, reflectively attending to understand, and empathically responding to connect emotionally. Assess the quality of your acts of listening communication. Please check insert an X below the number that best describes your response to each statement.

Item	Listening and Communication Check 1= Always; 2= Frequently; 3= Sometimes; 4= Almost Never; 5= Never	1	2	3	4	5
1	I empathetically listen to understand and be understood					
2	I reflectively Listen carefully to understand and be understood					
3	I Use positive words to help others build self confidence					
4	I Show interest in listening and looking directly at others as they speak to me					
5	I pay careful attention to what is being said.					
6	I listen to the expressed feelings even when I disagree					
7	I Look for the unspoken words when I listen-					
8	I am aware of my own weaknesses when listening to people's concerns					
9	I Avoid interruption and respond only when necessary.					
10	I am always willing to avoid factors that may hinder my communication					
	Add up your rating in each column					

Score Range	Guide and Explanation of Score: understand the areas you need to develop	Total Score =
10-17:	Great Listener; keep it up!	
18-25:	Above Average listener; need to work on 25% of the areas	
26-33	Average listener; need to work on 50% of the areas	
34-41	Below average listener; need to work on 75% of the areas	
42-50	Not a listener; Seek help in all the areas	

CHAPTER 3
DEVELOPING LISTENING–PATIENCE

Listening patience is an important catalyst that begins and drives the three characteristics (*attention, concentration,* and *hearing*) of listening communication. Patience is the ability to endure waiting, delay, or provocation without becoming annoyed or upset or to persevere calmly when faced with difficulties. Listening-patience is the patience or patient attitude that produces effective listening. Without an exercise of patience between the parties in listening, paying attention, hearing, and good processing to understand, real communication will not take place. A leader-servant strives to pay attention to what is said patiently, listening reflectively to best understand, and responding empathetically to be understood. Patience has been identified as an important character trait that directly impacts listening communication. The leadership challenges in dealing with several human factors in the workplace can be traced to the leader's character trait of patience. A good natural example is one from Nelson Mandela. He recounted in his auto-biography, *Long walk to Freedom,*[12] that his "notions of leadership were profoundly influenced by observing the regent Reverend Matyolo and his court." He reflected on how this leader would patiently spend hours listening to both friends and foes in a gathering of national and local matters, In a typical gathering in this court in Great Place, the regent would open the discussions with greetings and for the next several hours that followed, he just listened patiently as people spoke, often to vehemently criticize him. Mr. Mandela summarized this observation and its impact on him as follows:

"But no matter the charges, the regent simply listened, not defending himself, showing no emotions at all"... As a leader, I have always followed the principles I first saw demonstrated by the regent in the Great Place. I have always endeavored to listen to what each and everyone has to say in a discussion before venturing my own opinion... I always remember the regent's axiom: a leader, he said, is like a shepherd. He stays behind the flock, letting the most nimble go out ahead, whereupon the others follow, not realizing that all along they are being directed from behind." [12]

The scriptures make it clear that God is patient, love is patient, and you are *to "walk in a manner worthy of the calling to which you have been called, with all humility and gentleness, with patience, bearing with one another in love, eager to maintain the unity of the Spirit in the bond of peace."* (Ephesians 4:1-3) At the core of our ability to listen are humility, gentleness, bearing with each other, and demonstration of love when speaking with or listening to each other. In general, patience denotes long suffering and the capacity or calmness to endure a wait without complaint. Patience produces the effective listening ability to tolerate delay in one's turn to speak or respond when challenged, as seen in the case of regent in the above example. Here are a few practices to develop listening patience:

DEVELOP PATIENT-HUMILITY

In all of its forms, patience is driven by humility to think of the other person as equal or even better without prejudging. Patient-humility listening is one-way of empathetic listening as David expressed, "O Lord, you hear the desire of the afflicted; you will strengthen their heart; you will incline your ear" (Psalm 10:17-18, ESV). Humility allows us to concentrate, listen, and submit to one another out of reverence for Christ. Humility is the way we serve others and our reality and therefore links us to oneness, equality, and divinity all at once. Other qualities of humility that allow us to be patient in communication include the following: [30]

- Humility assists our reception in empathy by helping us to see the other person's need to be served or heard.
- Humility gets us out of our personal minds, out of our individual ego, and our perceptions long enough to let us see, hear, and sense what others feel and suffer.

- Humility helps us to self-regulate the verbal and nonverbal behaviors in interpersonal relationships in service to others, allowing our self-reflection to be deeper and more accurate.
- Humility allows us to recognize others and see them as equals; it allows us to be open-minded, decrease our sense of pride, and serve others by listening

Develop patient-emotional regulation

Regulating your emotion is a product of self-control and the ability to shift your perspective to that of the speaker with a focus and open mind to want to understand. Having the correct perspective will reduce conflict and anger that result when people are unable to handle the differences in their perspectives. It also involves emotional intelligence that allows one to regulate his emotions in order to control interrupting the speaker.

Develop a sense of maturity and respect.

Impatience in communication always results in irritating both the listener and the speakers, resulting in breaking down the communication. A sense of mutual respect and regulation of emotions requires understanding the impact of losing your tempers in listening engagement. When one person wants his way rather than the other person's, wants to achieve superiority, or wants to protect his own views, they are more likely to be impatient. In the end, nobody wins because, at the height of anger and uncontrolled emotions, nobody is listening.

Patience produces healing through listening

Most conflicts between friends or married couples are known to be due to pride resulting in a breakdown in communication. Opportunities for the couples to just listen, or be listened to, will often produce the beginning point to resolution. The same is true in most caregiving ministries. The opportunity for a trusted friend to just patiently listen to your life issues could be as healing or therapeutic as medication. Dr. *Rachel Naomi Remen, MD,* an author, teacher, and pioneer in integrative medicine, summarized it best:

"Listening is the oldest and perhaps the most powerful tool of healing. It is often through the quality of our listening and not the wisdom of our words that we are able to affect the most profound changes in the people around us. When we listen we offer sanctuary for the homeless parts within the other person...When you listen generously to people, they can hear the truth in themselves often for the first time." [13]

Patience in listening provides people with a great sense of inner peace, strength, and emotional control that produces effective communication and understanding.

A positive attitude produces patience

Positive attitudes that produce patience are those that encourage respect and demonstrate care and love for the speaker or listener. One such attitude is the ability to control or show no emotions even when reviled in a communication. The notion that two wrongs cannot make a right is true in this case. The positive attitude of one person in a two-person communication remaining in control of his emotions creates a pathway for patience. A positive attitude of displaying affective signs as simple as a smile, reflective questions to the speaker, and frequent words of affirmation can have profound effects on the practice of patience. Constructive attitudes that build trust and confidence create a sense of comfort and exercise patience between people to want to be in a communication process.

SUMMARY 3
DEVELOPING LISTENING- PATIENCE

Before starting this exercise, please read and follow the instruction in the preface of this workbook. Answers to these questions are contained in this chapter. Completion of these exercises after reading the chapter should take 60-90 minutes.

Discovering the Acts of Listening-Patience

1. Define patience attribute. What is listening-patience?; what is its role in communication?.

CHAPTER 3
DEVELOPING LISTENING-PATIENCE

2. Why is patience identified as an important character trait that directly impacts listening communication? .

Nelson Mandela reflected on how this Regent leader patiently spent hours listening to both friends and foes in a gathering of national and local matters, Mr. Mandela summarized this observation and its impact on him as follows:

> *"But no matter the charges, the regent simply listened, not defending himself, showing no emotions at all"…As a leader, I have always followed the principles I first saw demonstrated by the regent in the Great Place. I have always endeavored to listen to what each and everyone has to say in a discussion before venturing my own opinion… I always remember the regent's axiom: a leader, he said, is like a shepherd. He stays behind the flock, letting the most nimble go out ahead, whereupon the others follow, not realizing that all along they are being directed from behind."* [12]

   a. What are the key acts of listening patience demon-strated in this case?
   b. What were the impact on Mr. Mandela as a leader?
   c. How is a leader in a listening process a "shepherd" according to Mandela?
3. What does the Bible teach about the patience of God (Ephesians 4:1-3)? How does patience produce effective listening ability to tolerate delay as seen the case of regent in the above Mandela example.

Practicing the Acts of Listening-Patience

1. How do you develop Acts of Patient-humility (Psalm 10:17-18, ESV). What is the role of humility in the context of listening-patience
2. What are the qualities of humility that allow us to be patient in communication: [15]
   a. Humility assists our _____ in _____ by helping us to see the other person's need to be served or heard.
   b. Humility gets us out of our personal minds, out of our individual _____.
   c. Humility helps us to _____ the verbal and nonverbal behaviors in interpersonal relationships

d. Humility allows us to _____ others and see them as equals and…._____ our sense of pride, and serve others by listening
3. How do you develop the Acts of patient-emotional regulation?
4. How do you develop the Acts of sense of maturity and respect?.
5. How does patience produce healing through listening?
6. How does positive attitude produce patience in listening?
7. With reference to listening-patience leadership attribute, what take-away, meaning or lesson can you frame to improve your acts of listening-patience in a leadership process?
8. Write a commitment statement for plan to improve

CHAPTER 4
DEVELOPING LISTENING–CONCENTRATION

Listening concentration is the attentive ability to concentrate actively to listen patiently to and understand what is being communicated or transmitted. Communication through active listening occurs at the point of the interception of understanding words that are spoken, unspoken, and in the spirit. This requires attentive concentration. Words are interconnected to make meanings, and understanding their full meaning requires undivided attention. We will deal with each concept separately. First, let us explore the full process of concentrating, communicating, and understanding. Adler et al (2001),[13] in their book, *Interplay: the process of interpersonal communicating* showed that adults spend an average of 70% of their time engaged in some sort of communication; of this 70%, an average of 45% is spent listening, 30% speaking, 16% reading, and 9% writing.[13] The results suggest that most adults remember between 25 and 50% of what they hear in a typical conversation. Learning to concentrate means, learning to pay attention to words, with our mind focused on the meanings of what is said or not said. The critical step to improving our attention is to resist the natural tendency to respond too quickly rather than being quiet. Concentrated listening can be characterized by attentively paying attention and humility in listening engagement as discussed below:

Be an attentive-concentration listener

Attentive-concentration listening is the inner strength that allows a leader to concentrate on the listening process by giving respect and absolute attention to the speaker and what is being said. It requires an attitude of humility and recognizing the other person's values. "We must pay the most careful attention, therefore, to what we have heard, so that we do not drift away" (Hebrews 2:1). Attentiveness allows the leader and follower to listen and hear each other. When one party in communication has a hearing impairment, it is the care we show through attentiveness that speaks more than words.

Be humble in your listening engagement

Listening is the same as saying to yourself as you listen to someone, "Your message means something to me because we are the same, and I feel the same as you." The very nature of humility is to provide an open door for well-being. A humble leader does not usually feel the need to be above or below another person. "They do not engage in power struggles during interpersonal experiences and do not need to have the last word." [45] Apostle Paul writes: "Do nothing from rivalry or conceit, but in humility count others more significant than yourselves. Let each of you look not only to his interests, but also to the interests of others" (Philippians 2:3-11, ESV). A high level of self-awareness is important if we are to be good communicators as leaders. A leader's self-awareness enables him to be an effective listener by paying close attention to what is most important and fostering a deep perception and sensitivity to other people's issues and an excellent understanding of how to adjust one's behavior to relate to people positively.

SUMMARY 4
DEVELOPING THE ACTS OF LISTENING- CONCENTRATION

Before starting this exercise, please read and follow the instruction in the preface of this workbook. Answers to these questions are contained in this chapter. Completion of these exercises after reading the chapter should take 60-90 minutes.

Discovering the Acts of Listening Concentration

1. Define Listening concentration. What is the role of attentive concentration in communication?. What is the critical step to improving our attention in communication process
2. How can one characterize concentrated-Listening?
3. What is Attentive-concentration listening? Attentiveness allows the leader and follower to listen and hear each other

CHAPTER 4
DEVELOPING LISTENING-CONCENTRATION

Practicing the Acts of Listening-Concentration

Listening-Concentration is the attentive ability to actively con-centrate to listen to and understand what is being commun-icated; it occurs at the point of interception of understanding words that are spoken, unspoken, and in the spirit.

1. How does the quality of attentive-concentration listening allow a leader to concentrate on the listening process?
2. What part does the quality of humility play in concen-tration-listening?
3. How can a leader's listening-self-awareness ability increase listening effectiveness?
4. What kind of attitude is required in attentive-concentration listening ((Hebrews 2:1).
5. The very nature of humility is to provide an open door for well-being. How can we Be humble in our listening engage-ment. See Philippians 2:3-11.
6. How can the quality self-awareness enable a leader to be an effective listener
7. With reference to listening-concentration leadership attribute, what take-away, meaning or lesson can you frame to improve your acts of listening-concentration in a leadership process?
8. Write a commitment statement for plan to improve.

CHAPTER 5
DEVELOPING LISTENING-HEARING

The critical purpose of paying attention in communication is to hear what is being transmitted or said. Hearing-listening means patiently paying attention to hear the words with all of your ears, open mind, and attentiveness to understanding. It means paying close attention to the content of the word. We read from Hebrews: "Therefore, we must pay much closer attention to what we have heard, lest we drift away from it" (Hebrews 2:1 ESV). Hearing is the most critical of the three elements of listening because without hearing the words, there will be no meaning drawn and therefore, no understanding, and no communication. Lack of attention to what is communicated will lead us to "drift away." In listening to God, a leader wants to hear God, and in hearing His Word, he or she grows in faith and comes to know the depth of his or her love responsibilities in service leadership.

Hearing the word in communication is the beginning of our understanding not only of the words spoken but of the people involved in the communication. Hearing is maximized when a leader shows a reasonable level of patience and empathy; indeed, without empathy and intentional connection to a follower, it is hard for a leader to hear effectively what a follower is saying. Hearing listening can be characterized by the following qualities:

- Self-discipline is what guides the leader's ability to hear what he is listening to. Effective listening requires self-discipline to control the tongue, appropriate responses, and emotions that often can impede communication.
- Patience controls the tendency to interrupt the speaker or prejudge what the person is trying to communicate. An impatient attitude creates a channel to lose a part of what is being said.
- Initiative to hear and include intentional actions such as keeping quiet, not interrupting and avoiding distractions. These behaviors enable the leader to understand and be understood.

Here are some hearing–listening tips to improve yourself-discipline, patience, and initiative involved in listening commun-ication:

Be focused and open-minded to hear

Open-mindedness means keeping a simple spirit, being humble, and giving attention to what is communicated while holding back your judgment or opinion. It is being open to what someone else wants to say. This means we must be attentive to the words, and the exact meaning communicated in the words. "And your ears shall hear a word behind you, saying, 'This is the way, walk in it when you turn to the right or when you turn to the left'" (Isaiah 30:21 ESV). When meanings in communication are not clear, we must reflectively seek clarification to understand. This means repeating the word or statements back to the speaker to ensure what you heard is what was communicated.

Be a sympathetic listener

The basic elements of sympathetic listening are showing concern and feeling for the speaker's experience. The listener or caregiver first believes the experience of the care receiver or speaker and then enters into the experience by participating or walking along with the experience. The result is that the caregiver believes and actually feels the experience at some level. It is this ability to believe in and feels part of another person's experience that makes empathy attributes an important tool for servant leadership. We can sympathize by reflecting, understanding, and showing the capacity to share in the feeling and allowing ourselves to be used for healing. Actions to improve our sympathetic listening, include avoiding the following "negative listening habits" identified by Adele Lynn, a consultant and the author of The *Emotional Intelligence Activity Book*, include: [16]

- The Rebuttal. Listening long enough to formulate a rebuttal.
- The Advice Maker. Jumping in too quickly to give unsolicited advice.
- The Interrupter. More anxious to speak his word than to listen.
- The Logical Listener. It rarely asks about the underlying feelings or emotions attached to the message.
- The Happy Hooker. This is using the speaker's words only as a way to express his message.

- The Faker. Always pretending to be listening.

Be patient and humble to hear

Often, communication breaks down due to our impatient hearts that force us to interrupt each other as James said, "Know this, my beloved brothers: let every person be quick to hear, slow to speak, slow to anger" (James 1:19, ESV). Patience, when we listen, is necessary to implant the word in us. This occurs when we submit to each other in a communication setting and put the other person ahead of ourselves. To be patient we need to be humble and kind to the hearer. Our speaking must be with love and respect for each other, putting the other person first. Impatience in listening to and hearing each other usually impede communication as each person insists on his or her way. This often results in irritating each other.

Showing empathy through love can yield the required gentleness, humility, patience, and kindness for effective listening and hearing. As the Apostle, Paul said, "Love is patient and kind; love does not envy or boast; it is not arrogant or rude. It does not insist on its way; it is not irritable or resentful" (1 Corinthians 13:4-5, ESV).

Be in control of your emotions to hear

Negative emotions such as anger can block our ability to hear what is being communicated because "the anger of man does not produce the righteousness of God. Forgiving one another as we, 'put away all filthiness and rampant wickedness'" (James 1:20, ESV). Controlling our emotions is the beginning of self-regulating those emotions to allow the word to be implanted in us to build better relationships. Self-regulating our emotions also mean controlling our tongues. "If anyone thinks he is religious and does not bridle his tongue, but deceives his heart, this person's religion is worthless" (James 1:26, ESV). Even when a follower is an aggressor, the leader has the responsibility to bring calmness for a "gentle answer turns away wrath, but a harsh word stirs up anger" (Proverb 15.1, NIV).

Be a doer of the words you read or hear.

Doing what is heard in a 'listening communication' is a practical way of communicating your understanding of what was heard. "For if anyone is a hearer of the word and not a doer, he is like a man who looks intently at his natural face in a mirror…and at once forgets what he was like" (James 1:23-25, ESV). This applies that acting practically with perseverance on what is heard is an effective way to demonstrate understanding and for the hearer to be blessed as a result.

Be an effective communicator to hear

An effective communicator reflects God's love in hearing, listening, and communicating with a loving attitude. Jesus reminded the Pharisees, "Out of the abundance of the heart the mouth speaks" (Matthew 12:34, NKJV) A heart filled with unresolved issues with another is an unforgiving or ungodly heart and will likely reflect on those in the communication either verbally or through facial expression and body language or other non-verbal means. Hence, a leader must readily resolve issues with his followers that could cause barriers to communication. Being an effective communicator means doing the following:

1. **Speak the truth in love to the hearer.** "Rather, speaking the truth in love, we are to grow up in every way into him who is the head, into Christ" (Ephesians 4:15 ESV). Jesus said, "And you will know the truth, and the truth will set you free" (John 8:32 ESV). Table 6.1 is a guide to speaking the truth in love. Use Philippians 4: 8-9 as a test of effective words in communication. If the answer to any of these ten questions is no, then the words are not effective and should be avoided.

Table 6.1: Tests of Affective Words in Communication

	Tests of Affective Words	YES/NO
1	Are they true (correct)?	
2	Are they noble (honorable)?	
3	Are they just (fair)?	
4	Are they pure (godly)?	
5	Are they lovely (provoking love)?	
6	Are they kind (Caring)?	
7	Are they of good report?	

CHAPTER 5
DEVELOPING LISTENING-HEARING

8	Is there any virtue (goodness) in saying them?	
9	Is it anything praiseworthy to God?	
10	Is anything uplifting to the follower?	

2. **Do everything in love to communicate affection.** "Let all that you do be done in love" (1 Corinthians 16:14, ESV). This means exercising all acts of godliness with brotherly affection and love (2 Peter 1:7 ESV).

3. **Guide your tongues in speaking.** Being sensitive and withholding meaningless words, body language, and gestures that convey anger or hatred toward another eliminate barriers that can block communication. Words can be corrupting and defiling and can easily reflect bad taste to the hearer. If a word cannot build up the hearer, it is not worth using. The Apostle Paul said it best: "Whoever guards his mouth preserves his life; he who opens wide his lips comes to ruin" (1 Corinthians 13:1-13, ESV) "Let no corrupting talk come out of your mouths, but only such as is good for building up, as fits the occasion, that it may give grace to those who hear" (Ephesians 4:29, ESV).

4. **Love not by talk but in deeds and truth** (1 John 3:18 ESV). As the Apostle, Paul said, "Little children, let us not love in word or talk but in deeds and truth. This means being kind to one another, tenderhearted, forgiving one another, as God in Christ forgave you" (Ephesians 4:32, ESV). Put words into action to affirm love to the hearer." Follow the pattern of the sound words that you have heard from me, in the faith and love that are in Christ Jesus" (2 Timothy 1:13, ESV).

5. **Share yourself with each other.** "Being affectionately desirous of you, we were ready to share with you not only the gospel of God but also ourselves because you had become very dear to us" (1 Thessalonians 2:8, ESV). Spending time with your followers is one great way to share yourself with them. Jesus communicated a lot through parables but often found time to spend with his disciples to explain things further for them, as part of his mentoring, empowering, and revealing other inner and deeper meanings of this life and His ministries. "In fact, in his public ministry he never taught without using parables; however, afterward, when he was alone with his disciples, he explained everything to them" (Mark

4:34, NLT). On other occasions, after returning from an assigned mission, "The apostles gathered around Jesus and reported to him all they had done and taught" (Mark 6:30, NIV). This type of sharing with followers communicated love and care and offered Jesus an opportunity to get to know what has been accomplished, how the mission went, and any difficulties. It is more about showing care than measuring progress.

SUMMARY 5
DEVELOPING LISTENING-HEARING

Before starting this exercise, please read and follow the instruction in the preface of this workbook. Answers to these questions are contained in this chapter. Completion of these exercises after reading the chapter should take 60-90 minutes.

Discovering the Acts of Listening-Hearing

1. What is the purpose of paying attention in communication? What does listening hearing mean in leadership communication
2. What does the Bible teach about attention in communication? (Hebrews 2:1 ESV). Why is Hearing most critical of the three elements of listening and what happens when there is lack of attention.
3. How can we maximize the quality of our hearing
4. Hearing listening can be characterized by the following qualities:
   a. _____ is what guides the leader's ability to hear what he is listening to.
   b. Effective listening requires _____ to control the tongue, appropriate responses, and emotions that often can impede communication.
   c. _____ controls the tendency to interrupt the speaker or prejudge what the person is trying to communicate. An impatient attitude creates a channel to lose a part of what is being said.
   d. _____ to hear and include intentional actions such as keeping quiet, not interrupting and avoiding distractions.

CHAPTER 5
DEVELOPING LISTENING-HEARING

Practicing the Acts of Listening-Hearing

1. **Listening-Hearing is** paying attention to hearing the words with both your ears and mind open and being attentive to understanding.
   a. What is the critical purpose of paying attention in communication? How can that purpose be achieved?
   b. What are your five practical hearing-listening actions to improve your listening communication?
2. How can the following acts of hearing–listening improve your self-discipline, patience, and initiative involved in listening communication
   a. Being focused and open-minded to hear
   b. Being ga sympathetic listener
   c. Being patient and humble to hear (James 1:19, ESV).
   d. Showing empathy through (1 Corinthians 13:4-5, ESV).
   e. Being in control of your emotions to hear ((James 1:20-26; Proverb 15.1).
   f. Being a doer of the words you read or hear. (James 1:23-25, ESV).
   g. Being an effective communicator to hear (Matthew 12:34, NKJV)
3. What are some "negative listening habits" identified in the literature to avoid to improve our sympathetic listening?
4. What are some acts listening-hearing to be an effective communicator (John 8:32 ESV)?.
5. Use Table 5.1 below as a guide for speaking the truth in love. Use Philippians 4: 8-9. How many of these answers is NO in your acts of communication?

Table 5.1: Tests of Affective Words in Communication

	Tests of Affective Words	YES/NO
1	Are they true (correct)?	
2	Are they noble (honorable)?	
3	Are they just (fair)?	
4	Are they pure (godly)?	
5	Are they lovely (provoking love)?	

6	Are they kind (Caring)?	
7	Are they of good report?	
8	Is there any virtue (goodness) in saying them?	
9	Is it anything praiseworthy to God?	
10	Is anything uplifting to the follower?	

6. How can the following strategies be adopted to improve your communication:
   a. Doing everything in love to communicate affection. (1 Corinthians 16:14, ESV). (2 Peter 1:7 ESV).
   b. Guiding your tongues in speaking. (1 Corinthians 13:1-13," (Ephesians 4:29, ESV).
   c. Love not by talk but in deeds and truth (1 John 3:18 ESV). (2 Timothy 1:13, ESV).
   d. Sharing yourself with each other. (1 Thessalonians 2:8, ESV). (Mark 4:34, NLT). On other occasions, after returning from an" (Mark 6:30, NIV).
7. With reference to listening-hearing leadership attribute, what takeaway, meaning or lesson can you frame to improve your acts of listening-hearing in a leadership process?
8. Write a commitment statement for plan to improve.

CHAPTER 6
DEVELOPING LISTENING-UNDERSTANDING

Listening-understanding means patiently paying attention to what is being spoken for a full understanding of its meaning. The human brain is known to work significantly faster than the mouth, requiring the listener and speaker to self-regulate and control the thoughts and what the mount says to understand. Understanding is Habit #5 in Stephen Covey's *7 Habits of Highly Effective People*.[17] Covey recommends that we seek 'First to Understand', then to be 'Understood'. Listening, according to Covey takes place in four levels: One can choose to ignore listening by making no effort to listen, pretend to be listening by giving the appearance that one is listening, or selective listening by hearing only the parts of the conversation that interest you. Alternatively, one can perform "attentive" listening, which means paying attention and focusing on what the speaker says relative to one's experiences or "empathic" listening by responding with both the heart and mind to understand the speaker's words, intent, and feelings. Listening is a way to show that you care for others. Leaders self-regulate their listening attitude to understand and be understood as an act of caring and building relationships with others.

A leader-servant's choice is always to be an emphatic listener. The two important attitudes in understanding listening as an element of effective listening and communication are empathy and reflection. Empathy is a critical element of a full understanding of what is being communicated. Empathy is "an intuitive act in which we give complete attention to someone else's experience in a way that allows the other to realize that we both share and understand the essential quality of that experience."[18] The empathy attribute enables the leader to hear what others are really saying. The second attitude is reflection. Reflection in listening is another way of empathizing to understand the other person's experience and point of view by seeing issues from their perspective.

DEVELOPING ACTIVE LISTENING SKILLS

Set an active personal goal to hear the words in messages. Commit yourself to the goal to hear what other people are saying fully by setting aside all other thoughts and behaviors and concentrating on the message. The three elements to be developed in communicating with followers are, developing skills for understanding the words spoken (content), the unspoken (nonverbal), and words in the spirit (emotions within the words).

Understand the content of the words spoken

Paying attention to the key elements of active reflective listening will help ensure that you understand the words. This includes paying attention to word content (thoughts, beliefs, evaluations, etc.) to understand the issues. Giving your undivided attention and acknowledging the message being communicated improves your engagement in the process. The listener must reflect back the content to the speaker to ensure they understand. This is done by paraphrasing the key content of the message to show that you are interested and clarifying the message for understanding and correct interpretation.

Be empathetic and sensitive to expressed feelings (Luke 14:26, Hebrews 4:15). Strive to understand the meaning of what is expressed; be fully centered on comforting the emotions. If the issue being discussed involves a broken relationship, focus on reconciliation rather than resolution. Be patient and do not interrupt or be quick to dismiss concerns.

Another effective strategy for reflective listening is to show that you care about what is being spoken by looking directly at others as they speak to you. Even when the speaker pauses, it may not be time for you to speak. As leaders, we must show restraints and good examples. It is not a person who speaks the most words that show effectiveness, but a person that uses a few words of wisdom and knowledge to influence the desired change in others. "The one who has knowledge uses words with restraint, and whoever has understanding is even-tempered" (Proverbs 17:27, NIV). Respond to the speaker when only necessary with respect and gentleness asserting your opinions respectfully and without prejudging. Table 7.2 reflects an example of a leader's response to show understanding of the content of the words spoken.

CHAPTER 6
DEVELOPING LISTENING-UNDERSTANDING

Table 7.2: Understand the content of the words spoken

Examples of efforts to reflectively understand content include the following:	
Reflective Content	Examples: Response by Leader-servant
Thoughts	"So, you're thinking this would be a good time to change jobs."
Beliefs	"Am I right in saying that your beliefs and convictions are very different from your father's?"
Evaluations	"It seems to me that you really don't like what's going on at work

Empathize by reflecting on a person's point of view by looking at issues from their perspective, letting go of preconceived ideas, and having an open mind with the speaker. Here are two scenarios in Table 7.3 and Table 7.4:

Understand the unspoken words. How does an infant child communicate with a mother without words? The child will cry when he or she is hungry or needs some kind of attention. Imagine you are a mother listening to a little child or a leader-servant listening to a concerned follower

Table 7.3 (Scenario 1) Leader empathize by reflecting follower's point of view and feelings

Reflecting on speakers content and associated feelings:	
Speaker	Content and Feeling perceived
Leader–servant (Framework):	"Your main issue was (state content), but you think it was (state perceived content) and you feel (state feelings)." End with a responsive assessment question.
Examples:	

Follower to Leader-servant:	"I am really upset how he called me yesterday and without getting my side of the story he started judging me and telling me how wrong I was."
Leader-servant to follower:	"Your main issue was that he did not express your side of the story (content), but you think he was judging you (perceived content) and that made you angry" (feelings). Is that what you are saying? (assessment)
Leader-servant to follower:	"I sense your issue was how he approached the issue (content), and you feel he was judging you (perceived content). I am wondering if you were upset (feelings) because that was not the correct story." Am I correct or am I missing something?

Research work by Albert Mehrabian of UCLA, in his book, *Silent Messages,* and his research papers *on* the subject of non-verbal communication concluded that in communication, words account for 7% of the message, tone of voice accounts for 38%, and body language accounts for 55%. This means that the predominant form of communication is nonverbal—93% (38% + 55%)—rather than the literal meaning of the words (7%).[19, 20] To understand this 93% a gestural form of communication requires full attention and patience to observe and understand all the non-verbal elements, such as gestures, voice intonation, body postures, proximity, facial expression, eye contact, voice volume, and many others. These elements work together in communication to emphasize, empathize, compliment, and regulate verbal messages or sometimes give mixed signals. Non-verbal messages such as expressions of anger, joy, and sadness during communication can positively or negatively affect how the meaning of words heard is interpreted by the listener. Body posture which could mean how and where you stand can also influence meaning. For example, a listener leaning closer toward a speaker could indicate high interest while looking away from the speaker could mean rejection, impatience, or lack of interest. Nonverbal communication such as physical touches effective to the extent that the context is well understood. For example, in a funeral situation, physical touch will be understood to mean gestural sympathy meant to express comfort. A similar touch in another situation could mean and represent mixed signals and therefore must be practiced with care.

Some non-verbal elements such as gestures— movements of hands to convey specific meanings—are usually influenced by the speaker's culture. My daughter who was born and raised here in the USA visited some West African countries. When she returned, we had some fun moments comparing culturally-based dispositions. One of her questions to me was, "Dad, why do people in Africa speak so loud and with great passion." The fact is that most people in West African nations usually speak with high intonations, very aggressive hand movements, and sometimes pronounced passionate expressions in their facial and hand gestures. In other cultures such as in the United States, these are often misinterpreted as rude, arrogant, or yelling. People in the United States may use their index fingers to point to another individual while pointing with index fingers in many Asian cultures is considered rude. This means that 93% of communicative non-verbal gestures can be a challenge that a leader must be aware of and learn to overcome.

To be an effective listener, the leader needs to develop his listening-communication attribute to meet these challenges. Here are examples of how you can hear and understand the unspoken words (correct perception of unuttered words or feelings):

- Focus attention on the *spiritual concerns* (self-esteem, meaning, hopes, fears, etc.) to understand the issues; learn to reflect on the spiritual concerns.
- Look for the unspoken words: Facial expressions, tone of voice, and body movement
- Discern the unuttered words and what lies behind the words.
- Look for gestures, facial expressions, and eye movements behind the words spoken to reveal what is not spoken.

- Listen with your ears, eyes, and feelings open
- Listen to both the words and the ideas behind the words with the virtues of a mother's heart (Mark 10:45).
- "Listen" to the speaker's body language and recognize that nonverbal communication.
- Listen to the tone and volume to help you understand the emphasis of what is being said and the emotions in what is not said.
- Check your perception to evaluate your assumptions. Example: say, "Let me make sure I have this straight. You say that you love your wife and that she is very important to you. At the same time, you can't stand being with her. Is that what you are saying or am I missing something?"

Understand the feelings expressed (emotions in words). To hear and understand the words hidden in the speaker's spirit (the emotions, the hurts, the joy, etc. hidden in the words), a leader-servant can follow these suggestions:
- Be empathetic and sensitive to the expressed feelings (Luke 14:26; Hebrews 4:15).
- Listen with neutral emotions, focusing on the speaker's tone of voice and emotions in the tone.
- Strive to understand the meaning of what is expressed.
- Be fully centered on healing the hurt.
- Reflect on the feelings as much as possible. Why would you laugh when someone is weeping in the spirit or show apathy when the other person expects you to show interest?

ELEMENTS THAT HINDER THE ABILITY TO LISTEN

As I conclude this section, it is important to reflect on four key elements that can hinder a leader's or follower's ability to listen:

Subjectivity in an opinion: Watchman Nee in his book, *The Character of God's Workman,* defined subjectivity as "an insistence upon one's option while refusing to accept the opinions of others." [21]

Communication or the ability to listen to understand can be hindered by subjectivity. Subjectivity also refers to the notion of partiality in which a listener takes sides with the opinion that aligns only with his or her own opinion. Obviously, this is contrary to our model of servant leadership. The focus should be for the leader to listen first and try to understand the follower's point of view and then by example, help the follower to understand him.

Prejudice and blind spots: Hearing and understanding messages are also generally hindered by prejudice. Prejudging wrong or right before hearing the whole story is a blind spot, an unconscious attitude, or an assumption. Prejudice is generally caused by an attitude, opinion, or feeling formed without adequate prior knowledge, thought, or reason. However, at the heart of prejudice is a stereotype— a generalization of characteristics that are applied to all members of a cultural group. We must strip away stereotypes because they block our ability to think positively about other people. We must learn to listen and probe for differences in people's assumptions while suspending our own judgment to understand shades of meaning more effectively. Listening can also be done by building authentic and significant relationships with people you regard as different; this enhances personal empowerment. We must hone our inner ability to accept, move toward, or embrace different ideas and perspectives. We must learn to explore, identify, and value group differences by listening actively, openly, and respectfully to others and to frame every communication as a joint opportunity to build a better relationship.

Inclination on an issue: Inclination refers to putting a hold on one's ideas and emotions specifically on a matter so that there is room for considering another idea. Like subjectivity, the inclination is not an attitude of a leader-servant and can hinder his or her ability to be an empathetic listener. The same is true for followers. Through perceptive, nonjudgmental observation, and empathic listening, a leader must intently listen to the interests and concerns of others before expressing his needs and wants.

Speaking skills: A good listener needs good speaking skills. A good speaker usually has skills on how to deliver what he wants to communicate Think before you speak. Lack of such speaking skills can confuse the message and therefore hamper listening. Poor speaking skills will affect listening in the following ways:

- Confuse the message
- Delay the points and makes it harder for the listener to remember what you said.
- Detest the speaker
- Induce a lack of interest in the subject

SUMMARY 6
DEVELOPING LISTENING-UNDERSTANDING

Before starting this exercise, please read and follow the instruction in the preface of this workbook. Answers to these questions are contained in this chapter. Completion of these exercises after reading the chapter should take 60-90 minutes.

Discovering the Acts of Listening-Understanding

1. What does Listening-understanding mean? Understanding is Habit #5 in Stephen Covey's *7 Habits of Highly Effective People*. [47] Covey how do according to Covey seek 'First to Understand', then to be 'Understood'.
2. What are the two important attitudes in understanding listening as an element of effective listening and communication?
3. What is the role of empathy attribute in communication?
4. What are the three elements to be developed in communicating with followers?
5. How can one develop skills for understanding the words spoken (content), the unspoken (non-verbal), and the words in the spirit (emotions within the words)?
6. How can understanding the content of the words spoken help to ensure that you understand the words?
7. How can being empathetic and sensitive to the expressed feelings help in understanding the emotions and feelings expressed (emotions in words)?
8. What are the basic elements of sympathetic listening?

Chapter 6
Developing Listening-Understanding

Practicing the Acts of Listening Understanding

Listening-Understanding: This is paying attention to what is being spoken for a full understanding of its meaning. This means that to listen effectively, we must be self-aware of this fact and be able to maintain a considerable amount of self-control and concentration.

1. Explain how a person's subjectivity in opinion, prejudice and blind spots, and inclination on an issue can impede communication.
2. **What strategies will you adapt for developing the acts of Active Listening Skills**
3. How can we be be empathetic and sensitive to expressed feelings (Luke 14:26, Hebrews 4:15).
4. Empathize by reflecting on a person's point of view by looking at issues from their perspective, letting go of preconceived ideas, and having an open mind with the speaker.
5. Understand the unspoken words. To be an effective listener, the leader needs to develop his listening-communication attribute to meet these challenges. How can you can hear and understand the unspoken words (correct perception of unuttered words or feelings):
    a. Focus attention on the _____ (self-esteem, meaning, hopes, fears, etc.) to understand the issues; learn to reflect on the spiritual concerns.
    b. Look for the _____ words: Facial expressions, tone of voice, and body movement
    c. Discern the _____ words and what lies behind the words.
    d. Look for _____, _____, _____ expressions, and eye _____ behind the words spoken to reveal what is not spoken.
    e. Listen with your ears, eyes, and _____ open
    f. Listen to both the words and the ideas behind the words with the virtues of a mother's heart (Mark 10:45).
    g. "Listen" to the speaker's _____ and recognize that nonverbal communication.
    h. Listen to the _____ to help you understand the emphasis of what is being said and the emotions in what is not said.
    i. Check your _____ to evaluate your assumptions.

ALS Listening Communication Leadership
Attributes, Principles, & Practices

6. How do improve your Understanding the feelings expressed (emotions in words).
    a. Be _____ and sensitive to the expressed feelings (Luke 14:26; Hebrews 4:15).
    b. Listen with _____l emotions, focusing on the speaker's tone of voice and emotions in the tone.
    c. Strive to _____ the meaning of what is expressed.
    d. Be fully _____ on healing the hurt.
    e. Reflect on the _____ as much as possible.
7. What are the Elements that hinder the ability to listen
8. With reference to listening-understanding leadership attribute, what take-away, meaning or lesson can you frame to improve your acts of listening-understanding in a leadership process?
9. Write a commitment statement for plan to improve

TOPIC INDEX

About This Book, 22
accountability, 53
Attentive-concentration
   definition of, 69, 70
authentic, 24, 26, 87
authentic leadership, 37
Authentic Leadership, 45
Authenticity, 43
Comfort, 41
commitment, 19, 25
communication, 52, 54, 57, 69, 73, 74, 75,
   78, 79
   affective words in, 76
   barriers, 77
   example, 55
   hearing the word, 73
   importance, 52, 58
   listening, 75
   open mind, 74
   types of, 30, 51
Communication, 30, 56
   active listening, 69, 71
   definition of, 53
   with Followers, 53, 58
   with God, 51, 58
   with Holy Spirit, 52, 58
Comparisons
   with other works, 40
Compassion, 28
Concentration-listening
   definition of, 69, 71
Content, 55, 82, 83
credibility, 48
effective communicator, 76
elements that hinder Listening, 86, 89, 90
Elements that Hinder Listening
   Inclination, 87
   Prejudice and Blind spots, 87, 89
Elements that Hinder Listening
   Subjectivity, 86
Elements that Hinder Listening
   Subjectivity, 89
empathetic commu*ent*, 54

Feelings, 54
Spiritual concern, 54
empathetic communication, 54
empathetic communication, 57
Empathy-attribute, 28
focus, 55
Functional Definitions, 35
giving, 69, 74, 81
Hearing
   listening, 73, 78
   the word, 73
Hearing Listening
   by Self-discipline, 73, 78
   by self-Initiative, 73, 78
Hearing-listening
   definition of, 73, 78, 79
humility, 69, 70, 71
Initiative
inside-out, 46
Joshua, 19
law of, 42
LEADER, 28
Leader as Servant Leadership, 42
   definition, 25
Leader First., 23
Leader-as-Servant Leadership, 23
leader-servant's affection-attribute
   definition, 48
leadership, **25**
Leadership Attributes, 43
Leadership Inner Value system, **25**
listening attribute, 56, 58
Listening-patience, 61
Model, 23
Moses, 19
Navigation-attribute, 48
open-minded, 74, 79
Personal Outward Authenticity, 47
process, 25
relationships, 75, 81, 87
Self-awareness, 70, 71
Servant, 23, 24
Spiritual concern, 55

suffering, 52, 55
Sympathetic Listening, 74, 79, 88
Teachable Moments to Grow, 80
test
   for leader-servant authenticity, 46
   of essential elements of personal authenticity, 46, 47
The Leadership Influence-attribute, 41
The Principle of Leadership Empathy-Attribute, 28
The Principle of Leadership Adaptability Attribute, 27

The Principle of leadership listening-attribute, 56
The Principle of Leadership listening-attribute, 30
Timothy, 51, 58, 77, 80
Trust, 52
understanding-listening
   Empathy, 81
Understanding-listening
   definition of, 81, 88, 89
understanding-listening Reflection, 81
words unspoken
   definition, 85, 89

REFERENCES

[1]Greenleaf, R. (1970). *The Servant as Leader,* Indianapolis: The Robert K. Greenleaf Center

[2]Spears, L. (1996). *"Reflections on Robert K. Greenleaf and servant-leadership."* Leadership & Organization Development Journal, 17(7), 33-35

[3]Russell, R.F. (2001). "The role of values in servant leadership." *Leadership & Organization Development Journal,* 22(2), 76-83

[4]Russell, R.F., and Stone, A.G. (2002). "A review of servant leadership attributes: developing a practical model." *Leadership & Organization Development Journal,* 23(3), 145-15

[5]Terry. R. W (1993). *Authentic Leadership: Courage In Action*, San Francisco, CA, Jossey-Bass

[6]George, B (2003). *Authentic Leadership: Rediscovering the Secrets to Creating Lasting Value*. San Francisco, CA, Jossey-Bass

[7]Shamir, B. & Eilam, G. (2005). "What's your story? Toward a life-story approach to authentic leadership." Leadership Quarterly, 16, 395–418.

[8]Anderson, GL (2009). *Advocacy Leadership: Toward a Post-Reform Agenda in Education*, Routledge, New York, 41

[9]Yacobi, B.G. *"Elements of Human Authenticity."* http://www.philosophytogo.org /wordpress/?p=1945, Retrieved, July 15, 2012

[10]George, B (2003). *Authentic Leadership: Rediscovering the Secrets to Creating Lasting Value,* San Francisco, CA, Jossey-Bass

[11]Wosu, SN (2014), *Leader as Servant Leadership Model,* Xulon Press

[12]Mandela, Nelson, *Long Walk to Freedom,* Little Brown and Company, New York. 22

[13]*Rachel Naomi Remen, MD* https://www.patheos.com/blogs/itsallinyourdreams/2013/05/listening-is-the-oldest-and-perhaps-the-most-powerful-tool-of-healing/

[14] Adler, R., Rosenfeld, L. and Proctor, R. (2001). *Interplay: the process of interpersonal communicating* (8th edn), Fort Worth, TX: Harcourt

[15] Slamka, S (2009) "Humility as a Catalyst for Compassion The Humility-Compassion Cycle of Helping Relevance to Counseling , College of St. Joseph In Vermont http://compassionspace.com/sg_userfiles/revised_humility-compassion.pdf

[16] Adele Lynn, "50 Activities for Developing Emotional Intelligence" HRD Press, Amhest

[17] Covey, S. (2004). *The Seven Habits of Highly Effective People*. New York, NY: Free Press.

[18] Hudson-Smith, A, Robert, J, Coulton (2013), P. Digital Personhood: Creating and Exploring Digital Empathy, in a Grant submitted by Engineering Physical Science Research Council, EP/L003635/1. http://gow.epsrc.ac.uk/NGBOViewGrant.aspx?GrantRef=EP/L003635/1

[19] Mehrabian, Albert (1971). *Silent Messages* (1st ed.). Belmont, CA: Wadsworth. ISBN 0-534-00910-7

[20] Mehrabian, Albert (2009). "Silent Messages" – A Wealth of Information About Nonverbal Communication (Body Language)". *Personality & Emotion Tests & Software: Psychological Books & Articles of Popular Interest*. Los Angeles, CA: self-published. Retrieved April 2016

[21] Nee, Watchman, *The Character of God's Workman*, Christian Fellowship Publishers, Inc. New York

www.ingramcontent.com/pod-product-compliance
Lightning Source LLC
LaVergne TN
LVHW050025080526
838202LV00069B/6913